FROM MECCA TO CHRIST
A TRUE STORY FROM THE SON OF THE MECCAN MUFTI

By Dr. Ahmed Joktan

DR. AHMED JOKTAN

FROM MECCA TO CHRIST

A true story from the son of the Meccan mufti

© 2020 by Dr. Ahmed Joktan
Printed through Proclaim Publishers, Wenatchee, Washington

Unless otherwise quoted, Scripture quotations are taken from the Holy Bible, New Living Translation, copyright © 1996, 2004, 2007 by Tyndale House Foundation. Used by permission of Tyndale House Publishers, Inc., Carol Stream, Illinois 60188. All rights reserved.

Scripture quotations marked ESV are from the ESV® Bible (The Holy Bible, English Standard Version®), copyright © 2001, 2016 by Crossway, a publishing ministry of Good News Publishers. Used by permission. All rights reserved.

Scripture quotations marked CEV are from the Contemporary English Version, copyright © 1991, 1992, 1995 by the American Bible Society. Used by permission.

Scripture quotations marked CSB are from the Christian Standard Bible®, copyright © 2017 by Holman Bible Publishers. Used by permission. Christian Standard Bible®, and CSB® are federally registered trademarks of Holman Bible Publishers.

Scripture quotations marked NIV are from The Holy Bible, New International Version®, NIV® copyright © 1973, 1978, 1984, 2011 by Biblica, Inc. ™ Used by permission. All rights reserved worldwide.

Library of Congress Cataloging-in-Publication Data

Joktan, Ahmed, 1991–
    From Mecca to Christ: a true story from the son of the meccan mufti / Ahmed Joktan.
        p. cm.
    ISBN: 987-1-7345462-0-0 (print)
    ISBN: 987-1-7345462-1-7 (ebook)
    1. Joktan, Ahmed, 1991- 2. Evangelists – United States – Biography I. Title

All rights reserved. No part of this publication may be reproduced, stored in a retrieval system or transmitted in any form by any means, electronic, mechanical, photocopy, recording or otherwise, without the prior permission of the publisher, except as provided by USA copyright law.

First Printing, 2020
Manufactured in the United States of America

To all those who are persecuted and suffer because of our exalted Lord Jesus.

To my spiritual mentor, Bryan, who pointed me first to Christ; to Reena, my mother in the faith who sheltered me in persecution; to my spiritual family in New Zealand who nurtured me in the Lord and provided for all my needs; and to all my "forever family" in Jesus across the world who fulfill the promise of Mark 10:29-30, "I assure you that everyone who has given up house or brothers or sisters or mother or father or children or property, for my sake and for the Good News, will receive now in return a hundred times as many houses, brothers, sisters, mothers, children, and property—along with persecution. And in the world to come that person will have eternal life."

ENDORSEMENTS

Dr. Ahmed Joktan has told a story of God's grace in action. He gives insight into present-day beliefs that will give understanding to the non-Islamic reader. More than this, his book is a rehearsal of the kindness of God extended to everyone. I hope his journey toward God's love will be your story, too.
—Chris Fabry, Chicago, Illinois
Host, Chris Fabry Live on Moody Radio
Author of "War Room: Prayer Is a Powerful Weapon"

Abandoned in the hot Saudi desert for hours at the age of four by a father who wanted to make a man out of him, flogged before reaching puberty for making the smallest error in reciting the Quran, trained to hate and terrorize the infidels in his early teen years, being visited by Jesus in a dream, receiving Christ and committing his life to his Savior, facing horrendous persecution, Dr. Ahmed is now dedicating his life to sharing the gospel with his people and drawing them to a saving knowledge of Christ. These are but glimpses of Dr. Ahmed's life. But the book is more than a testimony. It is also an introductory course on Muhammad and Islam. The author, in graphic images, exposes the hardship of growing up in Saudi Arabia and the harsh persecution after his conversion. Dr. Joktan is now a joyful, hopeful and passionate follower of Jesus with a vision for his people. Do not just read this book;

take action to encourage this dear brother who has a God-given vision that we do well to support.

— Georges Houssney, Boulder, Colorado
President, Horizons International

Dr. Ahmed Joktan pens an excellent account of his personal story in his new book *From Mecca to Christ*. He documents his experience as a means to encourage and inspire his readers so that we can stand for what we believe. I can see this book changing many lives.

—Kevin Wayne Johnson, Washington, D.C.
The Johnson Leadership Group

The book *From Mecca to Christ* by Dr. Ahmed Joktan, born and raised in Saudi Arabia, is a compelling testimony of his conversion abroad and his harrowing experiences of persecution upon his return as he courageously shared the gospel with fellow Saudis and other Arabs in the Gulf area. It is also a shining example of the triumph of love in his heart for his lost compatriots, in spite of their cruel treatment of him. His founding of Mecca to Christ International is a tribute to his undying love for his own people. His book closes with a passionate invitation to join him in his ministries.

—Dr. Don McCurry, Colorado Springs, Colorado
Ministries to Muslims

I strongly recommend the book *From Mecca to Christ* by Ahmed Joktan. I lived through some of the experiences with Ahmed described in this book and can confirm first-hand the persecution he lived through! It was the highest honor to exalt the Lord Jesus Christ with Ahmed while he was in Riyadh and lead the homegroup of Bible discussions. Reading this book will give you an insight of what our Lord is doing in unreached places.

    —Charles May, Riyadh, Saudi Arabia
        Retired U.S. Air Force officer

Dr. Ahmed's book is heart-wrenching, and it truly demonstrates the power of God in a person to forsake all and follow Christ. Dr. Ahmed and I attended the same church when I lived in the Gulf States, and I walked with him through a lot of the persecution he suffered. I remember him driving 13 hours each Sunday just to get to our church in another country since churches are illegal in the Kingdom of Saudi Arabia. In *From Mecca to Christ*, you will see the power of God on display. I can testify that this book is true because I witnessed a lot of it.

    —Andrew Stewart, Louisiana
        Retired U.S. Naval officer

I was asked to review Dr. Ahmed Joktan's new book, *From Mecca to Christ*. I received it about noon today. Barring a few breaks, I couldn't put it down. It was riveting! It's now 7 in the evening and I am still thinking about what I read and experienced. I journeyed with Dr. Joktan from his birthplace in Mecca, Saudi Arabia, to his current location in the United States. Dr. Joktan was raised in a staunchly religious Muslim home whose father was, and is, a widely known and respected teacher of Sunni Islam. In trying to please his father, he memorized the entire Quran, the Muslim holy book, by the time he was thirteen. Dr. Joktan relates how Christ appeared to him in a dream at night. This culminated in his surrendering his life to Christ as the Son of God and Savior of the world. I followed him through his rocky progression through medical school and how his father and family rejected him because of his newfound faith in Christ. It was gut-wrenching when his own father held a gun to his head demanding he renounce Christ and burn the New Testament. I followed him through a number of assassination attempts, instigated by his family and government – the price of daring to leave Islam. He was imprisoned, beaten, tortured, and shot at with bullets. When I first met him a little more than a year ago, his face still bore the scars of previous persecution. His face likely always will. Through it all, his faith in Christ remained unshaken. From start to finish his story is permeated with grace, love, joy, and the presence of God. The book is tight, extremely well-written, and easy to read. Every incident contained is well-authenticated. They really happened! As a result, I take great pleasure in highly recommending Dr. Joktan's book, *From Mecca to Christ*, to any reader who wants to know more about how Christ is dealing today in the Muslim world. His story made me want to stand up and cheer. May it do the same for you as well.

— Dr. Ed Hoskins, West Lafayette, Indiana
Retired Physician

Author of "A Muslim's Heart: What Every Christian Needs to Know to Share Christ with Muslims" (Navpress, 2003)

Author of "A Muslim's Mind: What Every Christian Needs to Know About the Islamic Traditions" (Dawson Media, 2011)

CONTENTS

INTRODUCTION 15
    Feast of Death 16
    From Mecca to Christ 18
    My Goals for This Book 20

1 | MY BEGINNING 25
    My Father, the Mufti 26
    My Upbringing 27
    Mealtimes 28
    Abandoned in the Desert 29
    Memorizing the Quran 31
    Jihad Camp in Mecca 33

2 | "COME UNTO ME" 35
    The Study of Medicine 35
    Arriving in New Zealand 36
    English Class 37
    My Night of Destiny 38
    Returning to Saudi 40

3 | MY CONVERSION 43
    The Tall White Man 45
    A Follower of Isa? 46
    A Night at the Pastor's Home 48
    Jesus, I Come to You 52

4 | FORSAKEN BY MY FAMILY 55
    Beaten By My Brothers 56
    Will I Live or Will I Die? 57
    Noah's Son 59
    An Orphan on this Earth 60
    A New Beginning at the University 63
    Baptized 66
    The Bible Online 66
    An Evangelistic Website to Saudi Muslims 67
    The First Person I Baptized 69

A Trip to See My Spiritual Father 71
A Christian Pilgrimage to Mecca 73
Proving the Quran Wrong 74

5 | TORTURED FOR CHRIST 77

Muslim Evangelism 77
My Via Dolorosa 80
My Departure is at Hand 83

6 | A FUTURE AND A HOPE 87

A Scientific Breakthrough 87
A Sign from God 89
Life as a Junior Doctor 92

7 | 13 HOURS TO CHURCH 93

Home Churches in Saudi 93
Church of Jesus Christ 96
Too Dangerous for Church Membership 97
Weekender Conference in the USA 101

8 | PREACHING TO 22,000 105

My Desire for Seminary Training 106
Open Doors Everywhere 107
Satanic Harassment 109
An Indian Festival 112

9 | LEFT FOR DEAD 117

Face in the Dirt 118
Escape from Death 119
An Attempt on My Life 120
Resurrection! 122

10 | DISBARRED FROM MEDICINE 125

A Mummy in a Lab Coat 126
Born Again! 127
Facing the Lions 128
Earthly "Graduation with Honors" 129

11 | REMEMBER SHILOH 131

My Doctor Friend from India 132
Freedom Hall 134

Satan's Inside Attack on the Churches 136
Remember Shiloh 137

12 | ALL NATIONS 139

Arabian World 140
Philippines 142
China 145
To the Ends of the Earth 146

13 | BULLETS 147

Cursed Infidel 148
A Disturbing Letter 149
Raining Bullets 150
Alive from the Dead 152
Duct Tape Saved the Day 152
A Narrow Escape 154

14 | ESCAPE 157

Hunted Again? 158
A Visa? 160
Time to Flee 161
S.O.S. 163

15 | FREEDOM 165

A Chance for Asylum in the U.S.A. 166
An Act of Congress 170
A Wife From Above 173
Roman Citizenship 177

16 | DUTIES TO THE LOST 179

What is Our Duty to the Lost? 181
What Can I Do Right Now? 184
A Paradigm of Grace 185
   Divisions *186*
   Compromise *186*
   Grace *187*

17 | WHAT SHALL WE DO THEN? 189

Statistics 190
Mecca to Christ international 190
   US Evangelism 191
   Equipping Churches 191

Evangelism to Saudi Arabia 191
　　Social Media Ministry 194
　　Publishing Ministry 194
　　Medical Outreach Ministry 194
　Your Part 194
　A Final Word from Ahmed.. 196

APPENDIX 1 | ISLAM'S BEGINNINGS & TEACHINGS 197

　The Orphan Spirit of Islam 198
　A Religion of Peace or Hatred? 199
　Muhammad's Wives & Children 200
　The Influence of Waraka ibn Nawfal 201
　The Demonic Influence Over Muhammad 203
　The Death of Waraka ibn Nawfal..204
　From Peace to War after Waraka's Death 206
　Jihad 208
　Pillars of Islam... 212
　The Muslim Holy Books 217
　Sunnis & Shiites & Their Divergent Teachings 218
　Festivals...219

APPENDIX 2 | ISLAM TODAY 223

　No Religious Freedom...224
　Women 226
　Wife Beating 228
　Polygamy 230
　Slavery... 231
　Music Forbidden 233
　The Death Penalty: Beheading, Crucifixion, Etc.................................... 234
　My Devotion to Islam.. 236

ACKNOWLEDGEMENTS 237

INTRODUCTION

For God saved and called us to live a holy life. He did this, not because we deserved it, but because that was his plan from before the beginning of time—to show us his grace through Christ Jesus.
2 TIMOTHY 1:9

I grew up in Mecca, the birthplace of Islam. Mecca is a city in western Saudi Arabia, an oasis town in the Red Sea region, considered by all Muslims to be the holiest city of Islam. It was the birthplace of Muhammad (c. 570 A.D. – 632 A.D.), the great prophet of the Islamic faith and was the scene of his early teachings before his emigration to Medina in 622. Today, there are about two billion Muslims around the world who bow down five times a day, kissing the ground toward my home city, Mecca.

I come from a very prominent Saudi family. We are descendants of Joktan, son of Shem, son of Noah. When Muhammad brought Islam to my ancestors in 610 A.D., my tribe embraced him as Islam's first prophet. The people of Joktan eventually became radical extremists, kamikazes of Islam. Through many generations, my family has produced warriors for Allah, the god of Islam. In fact, out of the nineteen hijackers from the 9/11 attacks, fifteen of them were Saudi Arabian. Several of those were from my own tribe, which is one of the largest in Saudi Arabia. My father called these terrorists heroes.

On September 11, 2001, after the last prayer of the day, I witnessed my father rejoicing as he preached in the Meccan mosque on how jihad[1] is an obligation for all Muslims. This is especially true for those from our own Joktan tribe. I can hear my father's words even now: "Our jihadist heroes lifted up the flag of Islam in the United States and brought down the Great Satan to its knees! How important it is for all of us to follow their examples. We must take down all infidels until the name of Allah is exalted throughout the earth!"

FEAST OF DEATH

We slaughtered sheep and camels to eat in celebration of the 9/11 terrorist attacks. Instead of mourning the precious lives lost that day, I am ashamed to say that my family celebrated. They looked upon these attacks as a victory. Throughout Saudi Arabia they feasted as revelers at the most extravagant wedding celebration you could imagine with the wealthiest families serving food on platters ten feet in diameter.

Imagine boiling a whole camel in a pot twice the size of a whirlpool tub. Cooks waited until the camels and sheep were tender and then added an unfathomable serving of rice. The pot was so big, you could swim in it. I still remember the mountains of rice rising from steaming pots, with whole sheep and camels strewn about to eat. So much food had been prepared that day, more than anyone could eat. Much of it was thrown away.

---

[1] killing non-Muslims in the name of Allah

Saudi Arabian Celebration Feast

I can still hear the sounds of my family shouting, "Allahu Akbar! What a wonderful day it is! America has fallen!" The roar of AK-47s filled the air, mingling with their voices and creating a deafening cacophony of chaotic jubilation. In Saudi Arabia, it is common for men to shower the sky with bullets on days of great significance, like weddings. Sadly, on 9/11, every member of every family in our tribe felt more joy in the deaths of Americans than they had on their own wedding day. Hour upon hour, the night sky was lit up with tens of thousands of rounds, bursting overhead like shooting stars, exploding with great *POPS*, *BANGS*, and *RATTLES*, heard for miles around. It was the sound of war. And for my family, it was the sound of victory.

My dad saw this great tragedy as Allah's long-awaited answer to the many prayers and petitions he had offered throughout his life. He constantly prayed that Allah would destroy Christians and Jews, and their great ally, America. It seemed Allah had answered.

I was born and bred in this deep darkness. I look back now in horror and wonder at what darkness had blinded our eyes and filled our hearts that we would rejoice in the deaths of innocent human beings.

FROM MECCA TO CHRIST

My earliest childhood memories are of meeting people from around the world making their pilgrimage to Mecca. I had little idea why my city was so famous. Every day new foreigners would come. They brought with them strange tongues, trinkets, and traditions unique to their own countries. I remember seeing a pilgrim from Russia holding a matryoshka doll, also known as a nesting doll. The bizarre wooden figure separated in half, top from bottom, to reveal a smaller figure of the same sort inside; that figure separated, and it too held a figure—then again, and again—it seemed there was no end to the figures within figures! My father forbade me from touching it, as such things were considered idols, and Sharia law forbids us to own or have contact with such images.

My home life was far different in Mecca than in the typical American home. Most western homes have a father and a mother, whereas most Saudi Arabian homes have a father and many mothers. My father is no exception to this custom having several wives located across different cities. Each wife has borne many children, giving me numerous siblings scattered across our country.

My father is a mufti, a high-ranking Sharia law judge. He holds a Doctor of Jurisprudence degree and Doctor of Philosophy degree in Islamic Sharia law. He is a well-known and deeply beloved scholar in the community. He is a published author of many books about Islam and the application of Sharia law. He uses formal classroom settings as well as informal contacts through social mediums like Twitter and YouTube to spread his teachings.

As a boy, I would go to the mosque five times every day to pray. Starting at age two, I attended mosque school. It was similar to American Sunday school. By age thirteen, I had memorized the entire Quran and could recite it without a single mistake. Knowing the Quran front-to-back, I set my focus on my duty and my heritage to wage war for Allah and his messenger, Muhammad. I craved Paradise and all the splendor it offered and dying in jihad is the most direct way to obtain admittance. Jihad was my wholehearted, all-consuming desire until one night when Jesus Christ appeared to me in a dream.

How could the child of a powerful judge and leader in Mecca come to reject the false god Allah and embrace Jesus as Lord and Savior? What would it take for a member of the main tribe that engineered the 9/11 terrorist attack to renounce his loyalty to his heritage and kneel before the one true and living God, the Father of our Lord Jesus Christ? In this brief book I will testify—alongside many other witnesses—as to just how my blind eyes came to see the love of God in Jesus.

Before we begin, however, let me also say that some of the events in this book may seem truly incredible, almost unbelievable; but every event described herein, from my conversion forward, has been verified by numerous credible witnesses and trustworthy sources. Stacks of affidavits, sworn under penalty of perjury, were submitted to the United States government to assist in my protection when I sought asylum.

While some of the details of my story (mostly names) have been omitted to protect my persecuted brothers and sisters in the Gulf States, I have preserved the specific facts and context of my life's story, making it a truthful representation. The publisher of this book has received the testimony of a multitude of witnesses, notarized affidavits, as well as many interviews to corroborate the authenticity of this account: my very own testimony.

MY GOALS FOR THIS BOOK

My primary goal for this book is to first exalt the name of Jesus and to "give thanks to the Lord and proclaim his greatness. Let the whole world know what he has done" (Psa 105:1).

Every day that passes since I have known Jesus, I have felt the weight that the Apostle Paul felt when he considered the souls of his own people. "My conscience and the Holy Spirit confirm it. My heart is filled with bitter sorrow and unending grief for my people" (Rom 9:1-3). My prayer to the living God and Father of Jesus is that he would open the eyes of Muslims everywhere; that he would grant them repentance and faith so that they may no longer be blinded by the god of this world (2 Cor 4:4); and that "at the name of Jesus every knee should bow, in heaven and on earth and under the earth, and every tongue declare that Jesus Christ is Lord, to the glory of God the Father" (Phil 2:10-11).

Fleeing persecution, as I journeyed around the world, I came into contact with a wide range of opinions. I have heard what heads of state, university professors, and mass media in the West are saying about Islam, generally taking the position that Islam is a peaceful religion. I have talked to people who have confessed to being genuinely confused about the disconnect between the official narrative and the horrific news about atrocities perpetrated by the likes of ISIS or Boko Haram.

I am also fully aware that, thankfully, the radical Islam in which I grew up is not taught by the majority of imams (Islamic preachers) and not practiced by most Muslims. I am not ignorant of the fact that some countries around the world with a Muslim majority population have been and continue to be tolerant to some degree toward minorities of other faiths. Even the Arabian Peninsula was relatively moderate before the advent of Islamic Wahhabism[2] in the 17th Century. It is no wonder, therefore, that the question "What is the real Islam?" is one of the most burning uncertainties of our generation. Maybe out of a lack of knowledge or out of fear, it is a grand investigation that few are willing to tackle.

As understandable as the reluctance to tackle this topic might be, my personal background compels me to provide clarity on this topic to you, the reader. To accomplish this, I will need to take you back to the inception of Islam and to the life of the prophet Muhammad.[3] In doing so, we will come to the surprising conclusion that both moderate Muslims and Jihadists can claim to find support for their views in the Quran and in the life of its author, and we will see that it all depends on the part of the Quran to which they refer. We will also see that the Quran mirrors the life of Muhammad, whose personal journey went through two distinct periods shaped by different influences.

As much as the facts presented in this book are disturbing to some and unbearable to others, I feel they must be tackled

---

[2] Wahhabism is the most strict and radical form of current Islam.
[3] See appendices 1 and 2.

head-on that many might to turn to the truth that is in Christ alone.

My deepest desire is for all to find the peace and unconditional love that I found in Jesus Christ. Not sharing my testimony, although clearly safer for me in this life, would be selfish. God has given me so much, and I feel compelled to share with others the treasures he has gifted. In particular, I feel a special calling to reach out to Muslims, especially those who have tried to kill me. They are my people after all, and I am convinced that they have been deceived, and that not one is beyond redemption. If this book could only lead them to cry out to Jesus, he would reveal himself to them. If this book would only encourage them to investigate the claims Jesus makes about himself in the Christian Bible, he would open their understanding!

I also hope this book will mobilize Christians around the world to evangelize Muslims and all people who are without Christ and without hope. I pray true Christians will listen to God's command to "Go and make disciples of all the nations" (Mt 28:19).

In writing this book, I have relived much of my suffering, but I did so to expand Christ's Kingdom. I pray that my story is not just words for you, but that you will mobilize yourself to proclaim the love of God.

My final goal for this book is to encourage those who are suffering persecution around the world, especially other professing Christians, to persevere and stay strong. Islam would be dealt a fatal blow if Christians would open their homes and arms to those fleeing from the oppression, control, and darkness of Muhammad's religion. Light always overcomes the darkness. "The light shines in the darkness, and the darkness can never extinguish it" (Jn 1:5). If you are reading this as a persecuted Christian, consider my story and understand that there is hope in Christ. "In all these things, we are more than conquerors through him who loved us" (Rom 8:37, ESV).

When we suffer for Christ, our comfort is to identify with his cross and rejection. As Paul said, "If we are to share his glory, we must also share his suffering" (Rom 8:17). Our precious Lord said, "If the world hates you, remember that it hated me first" (Jn 15:18).

I know that, through Christ, all things are possible. He alone can bring these goals to pass. My deepest desire is for Christ to build his church. We know that "the gates of hell will not prevail against it" (Mt 16:18).

Dr. Ahmed Joktan, The United States of America
January 20, 2020

1 | MY BEGINNING

I have called you back from the ends of the earth, saying, 'You are my servant.' For I have chosen you and will not throw you away. Don't be afraid, for I am with you. Don't be discouraged, for I am your God. I will strengthen you and help you. I will hold you up with my victorious right hand.
ISAIAH 41:9-10

Mine is a well-known Saudi family, descended from Joktan, son of Shem, son of Noah. Most people think all Arabs are descended from Ishmael, but this is a misunderstanding. The truth is, there are two different branches of Arabs: descendants of Ishmael and those of Joktan.

My ancient grandfather, Joktan, is mentioned in Genesis 10:26-29 and 1 Chronicles 1:19-23 in the genealogy of Shem, whereas Ishmael is a descendant of Abraham, who received God's blessing (Gen 17:20). My tribe is known for being Allah's warriors in jihad, intensely committed to the beliefs of Islam.

MY FATHER, THE MUFTI

My father is a mufti, an Islamic scholar who interprets and expounds Islamic law and who studied directly under the Grand Mufti in Saudi Arabia. Muftis are similar in position to the cardinals of the Roman Catholic church, with the Grand Mufti being like the pope. Muftis are also jurists and are qualified to give authoritative legal opinions (*fatwas*). The muftis interpret and apply the holy books of Islam: first the Quran and then the noble book collections, the Hadith and the Sunna. It is their responsibility to explain the sacred writings to the common people. They legislate what is clean and what is unclean, lawful and unlawful. Ultimately, they arbitrate how the people should act in Islamic society.

Because of this high position, my father is respected and deeply esteemed. Not only is my father a mufti, he is also a leader in a particular brand of Islam practiced in Saudi Arabia: Wahhabism, the hyper-conservative Saudi strain of Islam that is often blamed for fueling intolerance around the world and nurturing terrorism.

My father leads prayers throughout the day and lectures in the early morning, just after sunrise. I can still picture him teaching vast multitudes from the Hadith. These teachings were often broadcast live on television and social media. Faithfully and with unmatched zeal, my father teaches the Islamic way of life, and to this day he continues as a public teacher, instructing the faithful masses of Muslims in the core values and applications of Islam. His students are technologically savvy, using various social media platforms to answer questions from Muslims inquiring how to live under Sharia law. Through these mediums, my father's words reach even those living in the United States and other Western nations.

He is so committed to Islam that he believes Osama bin Laden is a virtuous martyr and that terrorist organizations (such as Al Qaeda and ISIS) are carrying out the good will of Allah. Their ideologies are promoted in his teachings.

MY UPBRINGING

Wealthy Saudi Arabian fathers of many children from many wives are somewhat removed from their children's upbringing. And, although present in our home, my mother did not raise me either. Rather, my housemaid took on the maternal role, as is common among wealthy Saudis.

We had two housemaids in our residence: one from the Philippines and the other from Indonesia. Whenever I was afraid at night, I would not run to my mother or father for comfort, as my mother was unwilling to nurture me, and my father was often not home, dividing his time between several wives living in separate cities. Instead, I would run to the comfort of my beloved Filipina housemaid. It was she who would read stories and recite the Quran to me each night until I fell asleep.

Whenever my father was in town, he would lead the community prayers at the local mosque in Mecca. Afterward, we would have a family meeting during which my father would line up any children in need of discipline. I never wanted to be in that line. A wide variety of reasons could land us in trouble: saying a curse word, breaking something in the house, sleeping through early morning prayers, fighting with siblings, disobedience to the housemaid or a parent, and so forth.

Even now I can see my father looming over me as I stand nervously in line.

"Open the palm of your hand," he'd growl before striking me with a round wooden rod, landing it with a force like a thousand lightning bolts exploding inside my hand. "Give me your hand again!" he would demand.

Again, trembling, I would stretch out my little hand, awaiting the horrible pain.

WHACK!

"Don't ever repeat your disobedience again!"

Utterly terrified, I would run crying to my housemaid, and she would pick me up and comfort me until I fell asleep.

MEALTIMES

In America, the motto is "ladies first." Not in my country. Saudi men always eat first until they've had their fill; and only then, when the last man has finished, are the women and children permitted to eat.

Families in my country do not usually eat together. Before eating, the serving mat is placed on the ground, then the housemaids, supervised by the mother, bring out the food. Since the men eat first, I would have to wait while the savory aroma of the food drifted through our home—torment for a child. I tried my best to be patient.

When at last it came my time to eat, I would quickly wash my hands (as all are expected to do before eating) and then scurry to the serving mat. The females and children would gather around the dish in the middle, and we'd begin with each person saying, "Bisim Allah" (in the name of Allah).

At last, the time would come! Our right hands would grab a handful of rice, then a piece of camel meat—so good! In our culture, we eat only with the right hand since the left hand is considered unclean, and no utensils or silverware are used. All food must be *halal* (permitted by the Sharia food laws which are similar to kosher food laws). Whatever is offered to you must be eaten, as it is impolite to refuse food. Pork is not allowed, but there will often be chicken, lamb, or camel, served usually with basmati white rice. No one may speak while eating as it is disrespectful. If you finish eating early you may leave the table and talk elsewhere but never while the meal is in progress.

ABANDONED IN THE DESERT

One of my earliest childhood memories is a traumatic one. My father believed that every great man should be a shepherd of sheep or camels, per Muhammad's words in one of the Hadiths: every prophet was a shepherd in some way.[4] So, when I was nearly four years old, my dad sent me, along with two of my older brothers and several Sudanese shepherds, to the desert near Mecca where his sheep and camels were kept. I distinctly remember this day because the moment we got out into the middle of the desert, everyone turned and abandoned me, piling quickly into the car and driving away into the dark of night, leaving four-year-old me gripped by fear, screaming and sprinting after the car until the red tail lights disappeared over the horizon. I thought for sure I was going to die.

Terrified, I sobbed and screamed for several hours into the emptiness for someone to help me; I even wet my undergarment. What I didn't know was that my father had arranged the entire ordeal, just to mold me into a fearless man!

When my brothers and the shepherds finally returned, I was in shock, voiceless, exhausted, and nearly out of my mind.

---

[4] Sahih Bukhari, Book 55, Hadith 618.

They took me to a tent they had assembled in the desert and sat me down.

My eldest brother glared at me.

"A true man doesn't cry," he scolded. "He doesn't pee his pants. A true man is never scared of anything."

I looked at my brother, scared to death. In my mind, I replied, "If this is what it is to be a man, I want no part of it."

To my great joy and relief, I was offered water and a few dates before exhaustion at last took its toll and I fell into a deep sleep.

The next day, after early morning prayer, we watered and fed the sheep and camels. We lived and traveled for several months thereafter as Bedouin shepherds, moving our tents and our livestock from place to place, following the water and the desert plants to feed the animals.

While in the desert, I learned how to make a fire, set up tents, and even how to drive—remember, though, I was only four years old! But this is common in Saudi Arabia. In the West, you drive all kinds of cars and watch for stop signs and traffic lights. In the Arabian desert, almost all the vehicles are all-terrain SUVs or trucks, and you watch for quicksand and steep dunes.

Our meals in the desert consisted mainly of dates, camel milk, rice, and occasionally camel meat. We would also hunt for rabbits and chase after lizards. Some desert lizards are as big as alligators—and very tasty I might add: a delicacy among shepherds. If no food could be found, desperation would sometimes lead to hunting jerboas: something like a cross between a gerbil, a rabbit, and a rat! Picture a gerbil-sized rat with rabbit ears and legs like a roadrunner, scurrying about at up to fifteen miles per hour—that's a jerboa. Among rodents, jerboas are considered clean, as Sharia law permits the eating of herbivores.

MEMORIZING THE QURAN

Ever since I can remember and almost as soon as I was able to walk, I attended the mosque. From age two, I prayed more than five times a day. I prayed extra prayers before and after every required prayer and fasted from food and water two days every week. Each year, I performed the Umrah pilgrimage to Mecca, and I completed the more detailed and holy "Hajj" pilgrimage to Mecca five times.[5] By age 13, I had memorized the entire Quran without a single mistake, becoming certified after the required three days and nights of reciting, stopping only to pray, use the bathroom, or sleep. During this time, I was given only a small amount of nourishment (dates and water): a practice called dry fasting. My teacher believed that filling my stomach would make me lazy, and I would need to be treated like the Arabian horses—you cannot feed them too much, or they will become fat and lethargic, unable to run fast enough to win a race.

You may ask, "How did you memorize the Quran at such a young age?" I will tell you: through the threat of severe punishment.

Erring on one word, even by merely mispronouncing it, would result in a severe beating wherein I would be forced to lie on my back in an inhuman manner with my legs resting on a chair and facing the sky. Then, in front of all the other students, my teacher would beat the soles of my feet with a

---

[5] "Umrah" and Hajj" are both Islamic pilgrimages to Mecca, Saudi Arabia. Hajj is one of the five pillars of Islam which entails more requirements and rituals. Umrah is optional and can be performed in less than a few hours.

hose or an electric wire, a practice called *falaka*. Waiting for that hellfire to rain on my feet was torturous. Sometimes, this beating would take place before the entire congregation in the mosque, with all my neighbors present.

The punishment of falaka or "foot-whipping"

I would scream, but there was no sympathy for those who would misquote the Quran—none at all. The following day, I couldn't even look my neighbors in the eye because I was so humiliated. Even my family offered no help because from their perspective, I had done something very shameful. At times, I would crawl back to my home on my hands and knees, unable to walk due to the immense pain and swelling in my feet. I received around twenty beatings throughout the entire process of memorizing the Quran.

Once I became able to recite the entire Quran in Arabic without a single mistake, an extravagant ceremony was held, and an important certificate was presented to me: a high honor and confirmation naming me as one in a long chain of those who've memorized the Quran, dating all the way back to Muhammad himself. When the time for the ceremony came, my father allowed me to lead the entire worship service at the mosque with him and my whole family in attendance. They were so proud of this accomplishment because the Hadith says that the parents of someone who memorizes the Quran will have a crown of glory in heaven.[6] Sadly, after I began to follow Jesus Christ, my father erupted with great anger toward me believing this reward had now been forfeited.

JIHAD CAMP IN MECCA

With the Quran now memorized, it was time to learn how to wage holy war for Allah. Jihad is the highest honor for any Muslim. As a teenager, my father encouraged me to sign up for jihadist training camp in Mecca along with other extremists from my local mosque. When I arrived, I met people from across the world. We were instructed through videos on how to slaughter "infidels" through military training, bomb making, and hand-to-hand combat. In Islam, it is acceptable to kill any non-Muslim in cold blood. We watched extensive training videos that included terrorist tactics, beheadings, and an overabundance of Islamic propaganda. We sincerely believed we were doing God's will as we daily recited the Quran and memorized portions from

---

[6] Al-Haakim, Book 1, Hadith 756

the Hadith. At night, we would pray at length for infidels to be slaughtered and hope we could be the ones to do it.

I am sad to say that jihad was the wholehearted desire of my childhood until Jesus Christ appeared to me in a dream.

2 | "COME UNTO ME"

Jesus said, "Come to me, all of you who are weary and carry heavy burdens, and I will give you rest. Take my yoke upon you. Let me teach you, because I am humble and gentle at heart, and you will find rest for your souls. For my yoke is easy to bear, and the burden I give you is light."
MATTHEW 11:28-30

THE STUDY OF MEDICINE

After I finished high school, it was my desire to pursue medicine as a career, following the footsteps of the ancient Islamic scholars. My father resisted this path at first, preferring I dedicate myself wholly to the study of the Quran and its application to everyday life. He had always wanted me to follow in his footsteps as an Islamic judge and scholar, and his greatest hope for me was that I would pursue Islam to the fullest.

It was a difficult conversation to have with my dad, but I did my best to convince him that the most respected Muslim scholars often first pursued the path of medicine. My father eventually, albeit reluctantly, relented and blessed my career path though I could tell he was unhappy. Little did I know this decision would change the course of my entire life as I would study English abroad and there come to know Jesus.

I was sent to a specialized medical college with an Islamic emphasis so that after my studies in medicine had concluded, I might become an expert in Islamic law like my father, the mufti of Mecca. I went to one of the highest ranked medical schools in the Gulf States, administrated by the government of Saudi Arabia. To my surprise, however, my classes were all taught in English. Growing up, speaking English was forbidden since it is considered the language of the unfaithful. Nonetheless, joy filled my heart at the thought of studying medicine, and I accepted the challenge to learn this new, strange-sounding language.

My first year was preparatory. I took classes in physics, mathematics, pre-med, and so forth. Because I was so unfamiliar with English, this was fairly difficult. Imagine if you could not even understand "Hi, how are you?" or recite the alphabet—and now *everything* is in English! I was so thankful for the internet and utilized Google Translate quite often to decode my textbooks. The entirety of my first year of medical school in Saudi was conducted in this manner.

ARRIVING IN NEW ZEALAND

By the time summer arrived, I was so exhausted from scanning all my medical texts into Google which, to make it worse, more often than not gave me an inaccurate translation. Obstacles such as this led me toward a path to learn English in the fastest way possible: through 24/7 immersion, which meant I needed to reside in an English-speaking country. Ever since the 9/11 attacks, few countries were welcoming Muslim people, so I searched for a country that had a low level of reported assaults against Muslims. I soon discovered that New Zealand was open to people like me and did not even require a visa application for anyone with a Saudi passport. I'd found my English-speaking country.

Arriving in New Zealand was like landing on another planet. Once at the school, they helped me get settled and asked, "Do you want to be with a host family or live in a hotel?"

I declined to stay with a host family since they would likely not be Muslims, but perhaps Jewish, Christian, or Hindu. I did not want to violate the Halal food laws of Islam.[7] To stay pure, I chose to live in a hotel, which was really expensive, but at least I could hand-pick my meals.

Upon arrival in New Zealand, I experienced intense culture shock. Females wore revealing clothing, a far cry from the all-black and face coverings worn by women back home. Because of the intense shock of western culture, I clung to Islamic culture and attended the Islamic center in Auckland, New Zealand for English language classes. Muslim friends I made there took me around and introduced me to life in Auckland from an Islamic perspective, such as where to find restaurants that offered Halal cuisine, and so forth.

ENGLISH CLASS

When I arrived at my English language class, I encountered people from all over the world—people from France, Italy,

---

[7] Halal is the collection of Muslim food laws, like the Old Testament Jewish kosher food laws. Islam is very similar to the Jewish kosher restrictions on food (including no pork and the like). Halal also requires Muslims to abstain from any form of alcoholic beverage for their entire lives.

South Korea, China, Japan, Germany, Holland, and many other places. Male and female students were taught together in the same class: another first for me. I did my best to never sit by a female. Even some of my teachers were female—yet another first! And if those firsts weren't enough, they'd frequently play music during study times! Often, I would be ignored when I asked for it to be turned off.

MY NIGHT OF DESTINY

The summer continued until the holy festival of Ramadan arrived. In this strange, foreign land, so far from home, my Muslim friends and I gathered together to perform the festival duties. Near the end of Ramadan, there is a night called "the night of destiny" (Laylat al-Qadr). Whatever you ask of Allah on this night (whether it is glorifying to Allah or not), it will be given to you. If you decide to do good deeds that night, the reward is given times thousands—in other words, each good work is worth a thousand good works. "The night of destiny is better than a thousand months" (Quran 97:3). One may choose his or her night of destiny; it can be any night during the last ten days of Ramadan. On my chosen night, I read the Quran, chanting Quran 1:6, "Guide us to the straight path." Then, I performed my rituals and went to bed.

These rituals are extensive, even exhausting. For example, the ritual of repentance has many options. You may recall seventy different sins. Or, you can feel remorseful remembering ten sins from each of the seven main organs: eyes, ears, tongue, hands, mouth, stomach, and private parts. Another way to demonstrate repentance is to confess to Allah specific sins that you may have repeatedly committed. Still another way is by recalling the variety of punishments for different sins and ultimately resolving not to repeat them. One particularly important ritual is to recite the prayer of forgiveness one hundred times: "I seek the forgiveness of Allah and repent before him" (Quran 12:97-98). The Muslim believes that Allah will forgive if the sinner repents. Only after fulfilling one or more of these rituals can one realistically expect to receive absolution and forgiveness on the night of destiny. "And whoever commits an evil or wrongs himself but then asks for Allah's forgiveness, he will find Allah forgiving and merciful" (Quran 4:110). After all that praying, I had no idea that this would prove to be a "night of destiny" in a way I could never have expected.

Sometime after drifting to sleep, I had a dream so vivid and real that I can see it even now as I write, playing before me as if on a movie screen. Cutting through the stillness of the night, the balcony doors of my room suddenly burst open and through the rushing wind came a booming, majestic voice, falling over me as a wave as deep and high and mighty as the sea itself. Then, like a magnificent fire of pure light, a glorious figure walked through the balcony doors toward me; so bright was his radiance that I could barely look upon it.

His voice was loud but also beautiful and inviting. He spoke to me in my mother tongue of Arabic.

"Come to me," he said.

This majestic, otherworldly figure was welcoming me and inviting me to come to him.

I was terrified. My heart beat uncontrollably beneath my chest. Fear took me from all sides. Trembling, I screamed the only words that came to mind, "Where must I go to find you?"

The figure, draped in a robe of sunlight, was so near, right before my eyes, yet so infinite and glorious that he both filled and extended far beyond what eyes could see. He seemed untouchable, so far away and yet so near and personal.

"Go to the house with white pillars," he answered. "There you shall find the truth."

I looked away, and there I saw that an entire side of the room had been transformed into the house of which he'd spoken, rising impossibly but in perfect alignment with the small space, keeping its true size and scope. And then, just as suddenly as it had begun, my dream ended.

Heart racing and clothes soaked, I awoke, drenched in wonder and terror. What had I just experienced? Surely, I thought, I have seen Satan himself. Immediately, as I had been taught to do, I began to pray, repeating the Quranic verses believed to ward off evil such as wizards, black magic, and demons. Muslims living outside Islamic territory for more than three days believe they are vulnerable to satanic attacks, and because New Zealand is literally at the end of the world from my home, I was petrified that Satan himself had set his gaze upon me.

RETURNING TO SAUDI

Compelled by an urgent need to return to the land of Islam and there find protection, I called the travel agency first thing in the morning and attempted to book the next plane to Saudi. I offered any sum they would demand to get me out of this treacherous place, but I was told nothing was available for almost a week, and no amount of money would change that. I was stuck.

To encourage myself, I recited verses from the Quran, hoping they would somehow ease my frightened and traumatized mind. Eventually, I decided it was not a good idea to stay in the hotel alone. Satan might return. The best I could do was return to school and continue attending classes until I could escape. I even stayed in the school lobby after hours until I was kindly asked to leave; I was so desperately afraid of being alone.

Morning came the next day, bringing with it speech class. Like a language lab, the teacher asked us to speak in English about a recent experience. Some gave very nice speeches about going to the beach. Others spoke about the cinema. Then came my turn.

"What have you been up to recently?" the teacher asked.

Nothing was in my head except for my dream. I didn't want to discuss it, but I had to speak. So, I recited for the class all I could remember about my vision, concluding with, "I think I was attacked by Satan, and that is why I'm leaving for Saudi Arabia as soon as possible."

The teacher stared at me with amazement as I spoke. Instead of taking notes, as she had with the other students, she just stared in stunned silence. No longer was she a teacher; she was like an attentive and transfixed child.

When I finished, she exclaimed, "You have seen Jesus!"

I had never heard that name.

"You mean Satan?" I replied. "Is Jesus your name for Satan?"

"No!" she cried. "Jesus is holy!"

"You mean Satan?"

I could barely understand English, and I had no clue what she was trying to say.

Appearing frustrated, she repeated loudly, "No! *Jesus*! Satan is evil, but Jesus is holy! Come to my desk after class." Surprised and seemingly delighted, she ended class early upon the conclusion of my speech. I thought I had really offended her and wondered if she would go to the school director to have me kicked out. Then I thought, "This is good. This will be a faster way to get back home to Saudi Arabia."

After class, my teacher attempted to explain to me who Jesus is. I believe she may have been a new Christian. But with her limited knowledge of the Bible and my limited English, it was almost impossible for me to understand anything she was saying.

Finally, she said, "I want to introduce you to a man who will tell you more about your dream."

She wrote down the name of a Christian pastor and gave me directions to a church. Little did I know that this was the same church building I had seen in my dream, the "house with white pillars". I wasn't sure if I should go: this might be one of Satan's tactics, I thought.

Sensing my uncertainty, my teacher reminded me of the story of Joseph the dreamer, whose story is in the Bible as well as the Quran. Interpretations of dreams are a huge deal to Muslims.

"You are like Joseph," she said, "who had dreams given to him by God. You've had a dream from God."

I didn't trust her, so I left the paper behind and walked out of the school, mumbling as I went, "I am in no way like Joseph!" I was still convinced my dream was not from God but from Satan. I still had no idea who exactly this "Jesus" was.

3 | MY CONVERSION

But even before I was born, God chose me and called me by his marvelous grace. Then it pleased him to reveal his Son to me so that I would proclaim the Good News about Jesus to the Gentiles. When this happened, I did not rush out to consult with any human being.
GALATIANS 1:15-16

After my class, I wandered about the streets of Auckland in confusion. My mind was clouded with thoughts, racing about from every direction. Returning home to my family in Saudi was my greatest desire, but my flight wasn't for another week. So, on I wandered, hour after hour, until I came upon a neighborhood in which I'd never been. And then, rounding a corner, my eyes were snatched to the sky. There it was: the house with white pillars. It was more like a monumental edifice.

My English teacher had tried to direct me to this very place, but I had been so distraught and unsure of who to trust that I'd disregarded her instructions. And yet, here I was! What a structure! It looked to me like a museum or an ancient Grecian monument, what with its beautiful, towering pillars. And there, etched into the stone set just above them, were the words "Baptist Tabernacle." I had no idea what those words meant. With no cross on the building, it did not strike me at all as a church.

The house with white pillars

Slowly I climbed the stairs and then pushed against the door; it crept open with a long, high-pitched squeal. This was indeed a very, very old building: from the smell of old wood to the ancient-looking seats, this building had to have been over a hundred years old, I thought.

I walked into the auditorium, wherein many organ pipes lined the back wall. I was fascinated by this larger-than-life instrument, which I'd never seen, nor heard as much as a single note of its music. After a great deal of exploring, a young man approached, welcoming me and informing me that someone would soon be in to see me. No one appeared for quite a while, and I nearly left. But then, a door behind me slowly opened.

THE TALL WHITE MAN

Just as I had made up my mind to leave, someone behind me called, "As saalam a'alaikum"—a common Muslim greeting which means, "Peace be upon you."

What a surprise to hear this greeting from a Westerner in a secular country! Turning around quickly, I saw a very tall, very white man extending his hand toward me.

I shook it gladly and replied, "Wa alaikum assalam *(Peace be upon you, as well)*", the equivalent of "Shalom," meaning "May God's well-being rest upon you."

He said, "I heard you had a dream. Tell me about it."

Fearful and amazed, I wondered, "How could this man know about my dream? Did he get this information from heaven or from hell?"

I didn't know then what I know now: that God had brought me to the very same man whose name my teacher had written on that discarded piece of paper. She had contacted him before I got there.

Though apprehensive and afraid, I recounted my dream, telling him every detail to the best of my poor linguistic ability. I told him about the doors of my balcony flying open, about the blindingly bright light, more brilliant than anything any human could imagine. I told him about the glorious man: his magnificent robes, his fiery form, his beautiful voice, and his words, "Come to me." And I told him about the command I'd been given: to go to the house with white pillars.

"This was not a vision from God," I explained. "This was Satan! All hell is breaking loose in my life! But," I continued, "within a week, I will be leaving for the sanctuary of Saudi Arabia."

He listened intently and then responded, "No, you have not seen Satan. You have seen Jesus."

"Satan?"

"No, no!" he replied. "Isa!" (which is Jesus' name in the Quran).

The shock of those words nearly knocked me over.

"Why would Isa call me to come and follow him?" I wondered. As a faithful Muslim, I was already a follower of Isa since Isa (according to the teachings of Islam) is a faithful prophet of Islam.

I was thoroughly confused. According to Muslim doctrine, Isa would never appear to anyone in a dream. Islamic tradition teaches that the next time Isa appears will be in his Second Coming on the final day, at which time he will destroy all infidels (non-Muslims).

A FOLLOWER OF ISA?

Still, I was curious. This man had greeted me with a Muslim greeting, and he'd interpreted the figure in my dream to be Isa, contradicting Islamic tradition.

"Are you a Muslim?"

"No, I am not," he replied. "I am a follower of Isa."

If this interpretation was true, it would be clear that Isa was wanting me to follow him. But I pondered, "How is it possible that a person can follow Isa without following Islam?"

My knowledge of Isa came primarily from sections of the Quran regarding the end of the world, as well as the Hadith, which teaches he will come again, destroy the cross, and kill the infidels.[8] It goes on to say that the whole world will then

---

[8] It is recorded in the Hadith: Allah's Apostle said, "By Him in Whose Hands my soul is, son of Mary (Jesus) will shortly descend among you people (Muslims) as a just ruler

pray the Muslim prayer, acknowledging that there is no God but Allah, and Muhammad is his messenger.

My eyes were beginning to open. The Quran has many verses encouraging Muslims to question the doctrines of Christianity (Quran 5:18), and I had many. The tall, white man graciously answered every one of my concerns from the Quran, speaking with great knowledge and gentleness of spirit. Many years later, I would learn that he had been a missionary to the Muslim lands.

The Holy Spirit was working in this conversation to show me that the Quran was not reliable, for as we spoke, my mind suddenly started to see that the Quran had its own contradictions, something I had previously been unable to recognize, though I had every word memorized. A number of instances flooded my mind: for example, Muhammad was once peaceful toward other religions, but when he settled in Medina, his philosophy changed to "fight them all." Also, Muhammad declared his way as the right way; then later in Quran 34:50, he acknowledged that he could be wrong: "If I go astray, I go astray only to my own loss!" Another discrepancy I saw came from Quran 51:49: "And of everything we have created pairs: that you may receive instruction." In biology class the previous semester, I'd learned about parthenogenesis, wherein not everything is created in pairs. That is a frank contradiction. The Spirit of God brought all these things to my mind, and question after question fell from my lips. It was as if I had been blind all my life and was now beginning to see (Jn 9:25).

---

and will break the Cross and kill the pigs and abolish the Jizya (a tax taken from the non-Muslims, who are in the protection of the Muslim government). Then there will be abundance of money and nobody will accept charitable gifts (Sahih Bukhari Volume 3, Book 34, Number 425).

The hour grew late, and neither the pastor nor I wanted to stop talking.

Finally, he said, "We are having a very interesting conversation. Would you like to carry on our talk at my house?"

I did not want to reject his hospitality, but I feared a follower of Isa like himself might try to kill me when we got there. This may sound strange, but in Islam, the only certain way to get to paradise is to kill an infidel. Not knowing any better, I thought perhaps Christians lived by the same principle. Was he looking for a way to kill me so he could reach paradise? It was an easy decision for me: I declined and walked back to my hotel. Before I left, however, he gave me his number, and I contacted him early the next morning, after which I returned to the house with the white pillars and continued my questioning.

A NIGHT AT THE PASTOR'S HOME

Hours passed like minutes. Soon the sun had fallen, and the pastor asked as he had before, "Would you like to stay at my house? We could continue studying there."

"He must be really desperate to kill me and go to paradise," I said to myself. "Either that, or he is soon to die of old age, and he wants to end well."

Kindly, he insisted, "We have a guest room. My wife is there," he added, "and I have kids and grandkids too."

With that, he began showing me pictures of them.

So welcoming was he that I finally relented. In my culture, we never refuse the generosity of someone if they invite you three times; so, I decided to go, but I remained cautious and alert.

We drove to his house in his car, and I walked carefully into his home.

"What do you want for dinner?" he asked.

My nerves teetering on the edge of a cliff, I said, "Only water."

I was so terrified that he might poison me!

When it came time for bed, I went to the room they'd prepared for me, took the heater and placed it against the door and secured my barricade by wrapping my belt around the doorknob. Closing all the windows, I tied the curtains to ensure they remained shut. Lastly, I arranged the pillows under the blanket, making a decoy, then slept beside the bed.[9] I truly thought he was going to kill me. No one had ever told me that Jesus commands his followers to love their enemies (Lk 6:35).

Our third day of study together arrived, and our discussion continued. As soon as he answered one question, I would hit him with another; all the while I could feel my soul opening up as so many important truths about the living God washed over me like a mighty river. Slowly, God began to open the eyes of my heart to the true Isa: Jesus, the Son of God.

Up to this time, we had been studying exclusively from the Quran. Amid all my questions, the pastor floated one of his own, "What is meant by 'the Word of God' in the Quran?"

"Isa," I replied.

The pastor handed me one of the three Qurans he kept in his library, and we turned to Quran 3:45: "O Mary, remember the angel that came to you, giving you a Word, that you bear

---

[9] Five years later, my friend told me the purpose he had in asking me to go to his house was so he could pray all night for me outside my door that the Lord would open my eyes to the Gospel.

Isa, the Messiah, Isa son of Mary, distinguished in this world and in the world to come, near to Allah."

"This is an example in which Jesus is called the 'Word of God,'" he explained. "If I speak, my words represent who I am. Do you agree?"

"Yes," I said, "I agree."

Then he said, "That means when God speaks, his Word represents who he is making that Word holy, right? God is complete. His Word must support that truth. God is sinless, so too must his Word be sinless and perfect."

It was at this moment that the pastor opened the Christian Bible for the first time.

A Muslim believes the 66 books of the Bible are corrupted. At that time, the Bible seemed to me like a mere human novel.

"No, no!" I shouted. "That book will make you crazy! It's corrupted and cannot bring any good."

The pastor calmly insisted on reading it.

"It's important to our discussion," he said.

He opened to John 1:1 and asked me to read.

"In the beginning the Word already existed. The Word was with God, and the Word was God."

"Wow!" I exclaimed. "There it is!"

The pastor patiently instructed me: "Just as there are two eyes but one vision, so too are Jesus and the Father one God."

The truth this man taught me from the Quran was also in the Bible! Amazing! Maybe the Bible did have something to teach me, I thought.

He went on to show me how the Quran esteemed Jesus and demonstrated that the Bible was a book about Jesus. He explained that Jesus is the Son of God, and only in him is there forgiveness of sin. Rather than ignoring the Quran and going straight to the Bible which would have immediately forged a wall between us, this man used logic, with the Quran as a starting point. He led me step-by-step to see the importance and relevance of the Bible. Like the Apostle Paul when he addressed the men in Athens, using their own culture and ways of worship, this man opened our discussion with what I knew and believed and used that to lead me to the truth of Christ (Acts 17:16-34). He didn't feed me solid food, but like a baby, he offered me simple milk (1 Pet 2:2). Paul had the same practice: "I couldn't talk to you as I would to spiritual people. I had to talk as though you belonged to this world or as though you were infants in Christ. I had to feed you with milk, not with solid food, because you weren't ready for anything stronger..." (1 Cor 3:1-2).

I read page after page, experienced revelation after revelation, and pored over the Gospel of John with great curiosity and wonder, asking more questions than I could count. The Bible is truly soul touching, so different from the Quran.

As evening approached, we came to John 14:6—the words of Jesus: "I am the way, the truth, and the life. No one can come to the Father except through me."

At that moment, the pastor turned to me and said, "Isa came to you in a dream. He loves you so much. It is rare to have him appear to you. He is asking you to come to him right now. Would you like to repent and come to Jesus?"

I reflected over the past week and thought how much God must love me that he would want me to come to him. How could I resist him any longer? In love and grace, Jesus followed me from Saudi Arabia to New Zealand—to the very ends of the earth! He led me to this pastor who patiently explained the good news to me. This was no accident. This pastor had been praying and fasting with a group in his congregation two weeks prior to my dream, asking God for someone specifically from Saudi Arabia to come to his church and trust in Christ. I was the answer to those prayers. My eyes had been blinded my whole life, but now, finally, my eyes were opened, and I could see.

JESUS, I COME TO YOU

Overwhelmed by God's great love and grace for me, I surrendered to Jesus. The pastor prayed for me, and I called on God through Isa, my only mediator, to forgive my sins and accept me. How grateful I was that my mind was no longer blinded to the truth (2 Cor 4:4)! I was a new creation in Christ (2 Cor 5:17)!

Time flew by in a single moment, and, once again, it was quite late. I stayed another night with my new friend then rose the next morning to catch my flight back home, but not before the pastor gave me a gift. It was a pocket-sized New Testament. It had a beautiful green jacket, with these golden words written in Arabic: "The Book of Life."

"I will pray for you," he said, "but this Book will guide you."

"Yes!" I cried, throwing my arms around him. "This is God's Word! It will surely guide me!" But I had no idea of the power contained within this Book.

It takes nearly a full day to fly from New Zealand to Saudi Arabia since there was no direct flight back then. For me, however, it seemed like a short trip. God had saved my soul. For the first time, I had life and hope and unspeakable joy bursting in my heart!

I landed in Saudi and walked toward customs. The Bible is not permitted to be in the possession of any citizen of the Gulf States[10] living under Sharia law. If the officers had found my New Testament, I would have been punished severely, even potentially given the death penalty.[11] So, remembering Jesus' command to be wise (Mt 10:16), I hid it among my English books.

My heart raced as the customs officer began inspecting my luggage. Seconds felt like ages as I watched potentially hostile hands combing so near to my concealed condemnation. I closed my eyes and prayed for the God of all truth to come to my aid. And, by his grace, my New Testament passed through customs undetected.

I couldn't wait to dive into the true Book of Life and learn more about my Savior, the true Isa. In the Quran, there is an upside down, shady, dark version of Isa; but now I saw his true face. I studied in the New Testament every morning before my medical school classes, learning more and more about who God is and what Jesus had done for me.

Though I was home, living my normal life and attending the mosque, things were no longer the same. I could never again see the Quran or the words of the imam (similar to a local pastor) as I once had. My eyes had been opened, and I could see that the Quran was from man, contradicting the Bible. Even in prayer times, when the imam would pray and

---

[10] The Gulf States are the Arab states of the Persian Gulf: Bahrain, Iraq, Kuwait, Oman, Qatar, Saudi Arabia and the United Arab Emirates. They function similarly to the European Union, only instead of a constitution, they live under the Quran and Sharia law.
[11] See the following article, which explains the death penalty for having religious materials other than those sympathetic to Islam. Mena Habeeb, "Saudi Arabia Warns: Execution of Those Carrying Drugs or the Gospel" (Cairo, Egypt: Copts United, 19 Nov 2014), online article accessed 4 Jan 2018. https://www.coptstoday.com/Copts-News/Detail.php?Id=89530.

teach the Quran, I was testing the Quran by God's Word and his Spirit living in me. How could I have ever been so blind? I had fallen for a lie! The beliefs I'd once held as so sweet became bitter, for like the Psalmist, I had now found God's words to be sweeter than honey (Psa 119:103).

My spiritual blindness now removed; I was completely free in Jesus. "If the Son sets you free, you will be free indeed" (Jn 8:36, ESV). "The Spirit alone gives eternal life. Human effort accomplishes nothing. And the very words I have spoken to you are spirit and life" (Jn 6:63). I couldn't stop reading my New Testament. The life of Christ was dwelling in me; his words were my food and drink, day and night (Psa 1:2-3).

The Book of Life (Arabic New Testament)

4 | FORSAKEN BY MY FAMILY

Don't imagine that I came to bring peace to the earth! I came not to bring peace, but a sword. I have come to set a man against his father, a daughter against her mother, and a daughter-in-law against her mother-in-law. Your enemies will be right in your own household! If you love your father or mother more than you love me, you are not worthy of being mine; or if you love your son or daughter more than me, you are not worthy of being mine. If you refuse to take up your cross and follow me, you are not worthy of being mine. If you cling to your life, you will lose it; but if you give up your life for me, you will find it.
MATTHEW 10:34-39

I continued living in my home in Saudi Arabia while attending medical school. As you might imagine, med school is quite challenging and academically rigorous, especially for a Saudi person reading all his course materials in English. A person preparing to be a doctor must read and memorize many long, extensively detailed, and not exactly exhilarating textbooks. This was a struggle because now that I was a Christian, the only book I wanted to read was my New Testament, and the only thing I wanted to memorize were words sweeter than honey (Psa 119:103)!

I desired to meditate on it day and night when I was supposed to be focusing on my medical studies. The New Testament drew me in, and there I found my joy, like a desperately thirsty person finding a well overflowing with delicious, refreshing water. After reading, I would hide my precious treasure, sometimes in the desk among my textbooks and sometimes under my pillow. I was in school for medicine, but my greatest joy came in studying the Gospel.

BEATEN BY MY BROTHERS

As you can imagine, my life as a medical student was terribly busy. One day, distracted by an upcoming exam, I neglected to put my little Book of Life back in a safe place. After my exam I went back to my room. I was about to take off my lab coat when the door suddenly burst open. In charged several of my brothers who rushed toward me and tackled me as if I was a criminal or intruder.

Within seconds, I was on the ground taking vicious blows from all sides. Lying there, unable to escape, while every part of my body screamed in agony, all I could think was that I was glad to have the exam behind me. My brothers said nothing as they beat me, refusing to answer my pleas for mercy or tell me what I had done to offend them.

When at last their fists had ceased to fly, they dragged me from my room on the second floor of our beautiful home to a secure tent just outside. It was a very modern Arabian tent, completely different than the one we used for camping as a child. It was like a guest house with climate control, a bathroom, concrete walls, and a fireplace. They hurled me inside and locked the door, leaving without a word. As the pain throbbed throughout my body, I sunk slowly into my thoughts where I settled into a deep pool of anxiety and worry—I hadn't yet reached the part of the New Testament in which Paul instructs us not to worry (Phil 4:6-7).

Our Filipina housemaid stopped by my lonely tent once a day to give me a hot meal.

"What did I do?" I asked her.

She remained silent.

"You have brought me up since I was just a little child," I pleaded. "Why won't you answer me?"

Very cautiously she spoke. Apparently, another housemaid had come to clean my room, and she found my New Testament. Thinking it looked interesting, she picked it up and quickly recognized it as a Christian Bible. She immediately took it to my mother who was shocked to her core when she saw it.

"This is an emergency!" my mother declared. "This Bible is not allowed in Saudi Arabia! How on earth did this reach my son's desk?"

To find a Bible in the house of a well-known Islamic scholar is very serious, and it had been my mother who had instructed my brothers to give me a severe beating and put me under house arrest.

WILL I LIVE OR WILL I DIE?

Once the housemaid had explained these things to me, fear took over my heart and mind. My father was out of town at the time, but the situation was so serious that when he received word, he immediately abandoned his religious duties and made his way back home. The gravity of the situation, and the panic gripping my whole family cannot be overstated. My father called for my brothers, and together they came into the tent, my father holding an AK-47 assault rifle. He placed the loaded barrel against my forehead; I was on my knees, trembling. He then threw the green Book of Life onto the ground in front of me. I can still hear the thud of that precious book hitting the ground, the dust from the sand rising like a mini explosion.

"Do you think you can shame me in front of our family, our tribe, and our Muslim nation?" he snarled. "I will not allow it! If you don't recant and burn this evil book you brought from overseas, I'll put these 30 bullets into your head!" It is completely legal under Sharia law for a father to execute a child for apostasy from Islam.

He released the gun's safety. Its familiar *click* sound, remembered from my time at training camps, hit my heart as if he'd pulled the trigger. Death lurked less than half an inch away from my face. I was shaking like a leaf caught in a hurricane, clinging desperately to its branch I felt I had no choice.

My father was so close to ending my life that I blurted out, "I'm a Muslim!"

Saying this doesn't actually make me a follower of Islam. Belief is in the heart. "Muslim" means "submitted to God," and I was the only one in that room that was submitted to the one true and living God, revealed in the Bible through his Son Jesus Christ. I am not responsible for my father's understanding, but I am accountable for what I say from my heart. I must be wise and obedient to Jesus. Like the Apostle Thomas, I was submitted to Jesus, my Lord and my God (Jn 20:28).

My father commanded me to burn the precious green book. Knowing it was only paper and ink, I took the New Testament, placed it in the fireplace, and watched the flames slowly devour it.

Then my father left.

Eid al Adha (The Festival of Sacrifice) came a few days later. Everyone was celebrating, reveling in happiness and joy, while I sat alone, a prisoner in my own home because of the Word of God. I felt certain my days were soon to end—would I be sentenced to die in the city square, there to be beheaded? Or would my father choose to shoot me right here? My thoughts were spinning out of control.

NOAH'S SON

After a week of endless anxiety and fear, I had reached the brink of hopelessness. Then, one day, as I prayed to the God of the universe to intervene, my father burst through the door, along with all the men of my family's clan; today they would decide my fate. As they stepped toward me, I recalled the moment of my conversion when I'd read the words of Jesus: "I am the way, the truth, and the life" (Jn 14:6). I called out to Jesus and cast my cares and fears upon him.

Just before entering, I could hear my father outside, chanting verses from the Quran, reciting the ominous tale of Noah's forsaken son. The story of Noah in the Quran is so very different than the one in the Christian Bible. Both speak of God telling Noah he will spare his family, but the Quran tells another story about one of Noah's sons, one who didn't take refuge with the others in the ark.

Noah says, "Son, come ride with us and don't be with the drowning ones. They are unbelievers."

"Father," his son replies, "I'll go to the mountain, and the mountain will shelter me from the water."

"Son! There is nothing that can shelter you today from God's (Allah's) decree, which is the flood. You can be protected only if you come into the ark and receive his mercy and forgiveness."

The waves then separate Noah and his precious son, who perishes in the flood. Noah then turns to Allah and says, "My Lord, indeed my son is my family. I thought your promise to protect my family was true. You are the most just of judges. How could this happen?"

And Allah replies, "This is not your son. This child is a bad deed whose life was not righteous. Don't talk to me about things you don't understand" (*see* Quran 11:41-47).

AN ORPHAN ON THIS EARTH

My father turned to me, looked me square the eye, and disowned me, renouncing me as his son that day.

"You are not my son. You are a bad deed. You are a shame upon me and upon Joktan (our family's tribe) until the Day of Judgment."

Then he spat in my face as a sign of deep shame and disappointment, and my brothers seized me and literally threw me out of the tent. I no longer had a home. I no longer had a family. I was dead.

My whole family rejected me—my father, my mother, everyone; I believe they even had a funeral for me some time later. After that day, I never saw their faces again.

My culture is one of shame and honor. Even my mother was not permitted to cry because the Quran forbids any emotions toward those who apostatize from Islam, even if it is one's own child. I was now an orphan on this earth.

Why was this happening? I had been so happy as a new Christian. Now I was ripped apart, utterly shocked, and lost in horrified amazement. God had been nurturing my soul with his Word and Spirit, and now my whole life was in pieces. As I walked that painful and slow walk away from the only home I'd ever known, memories of happier days flooded my dejected and stunned mind, eventually wandering back to my prestigious childhood. My father had carefully instructed me in the teachings of Islam. He had been so proud when I'd memorized the Quran at so early an age. I thought about the big ceremony when I'd been officially certified, and how he had let me lead in prayer at the mosque, the highest honor for a young man.

Profoundly traumatized, I wandered the streets, looking for an abandoned building in which to take shelter.

"What have I done?" I said to myself, drowning in ever-flowing tears. "I am now cut off, abandoned, and completely on my own."

I was in disbelief, terrified, and lost in a depressed stupor. The reality of being forever rejected by my family was just too much to accept.

Several old abandoned shacks, infested with snakes and scorpions, provided shelter for the next few days. In the darkness, I could hear the snakes hissing, slithering near me. I could see scorpion shadows crawling around and feel cockroaches climbing all over me, looking for shelter in my stinking clothes. But I didn't care. I just wanted to die. These shacks were so much like a rotting coffin. I felt like I was at my own funeral. Though it had been my family declaring *me* dead, I grieved as though *they* had died.

Day and night blended together. Extreme waves of disbelief crashed over me while tangled thoughts twisted about in my head. Adrenaline pounded painfully through my heart, causing me to hyperventilate and rendering me unable to breathe. Thereafter, I would be so numb and emotionally exhausted that I wondered if I were indeed dead.

"Who will care for me?" I wondered. "Who will be my father? There is no adoption in Islam."

I had not yet come to learn of God's promise of a forever family, the thousands of brothers and sisters spread all over the earth making up Christ's church.

After days of delirium, soundness of mind slowly returned and I at last recognized my decaying state, having had no food or water. Unable to stand, I crawled toward the daylight, crunching roaches under my hands and knees as I went. I was so weak, just pulling my feeble frame across the floor felt like dragging a jumbo jet. When at last I'd reached the road, a kind person saw me and stopped his car.

"Are you ok?" he exclaimed, rushing to my side.

I hadn't the strength to speak.

The man rushed back to his car and returned with a bottle of water which he then dribbled into my mouth before giving me the whole bottle and the clothes off his back. He must have just returned from shopping for he also gave me a bag full of canned food.

He then asked if he could give me a ride home. All at once, the tears began to flow.

"I have no home anymore," I cried.

The man looked on me with pity and opening his wallet, he gave me some money then drove away. I rose from my knees and put on the clean garment the man had so generously given me; because he had been rather tall and much larger than me, the clothing hung loose, but I didn't care. I then leaned against the wall and slowly began to eat, praising God for having sent such a tender-hearted person; that man was like an angel. Maybe he was (Heb 13:2)!

I slept quite a long time thereafter and awoke with renewed energy. Just then an idea came to my mind: I don't have to live as a homeless person. The kingdom of oil is overflowing with riches, offering all its citizens free room and board with tuition to any public university in the Gulf States, as well as a generous monthly stipend. Quickly shuffling like a penguin in my oversized clothing toward the main street, I hailed a taxi to take me to the university and my new home in the college dorms.

Looking back on the confusion of this time in my life, I think of the words of Jeremiah: "The thought of my suffering and homelessness is bitter beyond words. I will never forget this awful time, as I grieve over my loss. Yet I still dare to hope when I remember this: The faithful love of the Lord never ends! His mercies never cease. Great is his faithfulness; his mercies begin afresh each morning. I say to myself, 'The Lord is my inheritance; therefore, I will hope in him!'" (Lam 3:19-24).

A NEW BEGINNING AT THE UNIVERSITY

By the grace of God, I was able to move into the dorms and even postpone a semester of medical school. I did not explain to the administration the reasons surrounding my need for a break; I was shattered and needed time to adjust to this new, difficult reality.

During this time of emotional recovery, I discovered that I could read the Word of God online. Christian sites are blocked in Saudi Arabia, but extensive Google searching helped me find a way around this. Truly, a whole new world was opening up to me, and God used this semester to train me in his Word. No longer had I just the New Testament—I had the entire 66 books of the Christian Bible! This was amazing! A favorite verse discovered in this time became my own personal Christian 9-1-1: "Those who live in the shelter of the Most High will find rest in the shadow of the Almighty. This I declare about the Lord: he alone is my refuge, my place of safety; he is my God, and I trust him" (Psa 91:1-2).

While Mecca is the holiest city in Islam, my new residence at the university was another major center of radical Islam in Saudi. Most importantly, I had become a resident and citizen of my true home in heaven. God was healing my broken heart. Though I had been rejected on this earth, I took comfort knowing that my Lord Jesus had been rejected also: "He came to his own, and his own people did not receive him" (Jn 1:11, ESV). Like Jesus, I am a stranger and an exile on this earth. This world is not my home anyway. I am a "citizen of heaven" (1 Pet 1:1; Phil 3:20). Though I am dead to my family, I have these living words that touch the depths of my soul and mind. The Bible is so pure in its theology! It's so different from Quranic verses which are dead and empty. The words of the god of Islam are those of an angry demon. They are evil and relate nothing but death to my soul. The Christian Bible is alive! But how could such an awesome and amazing book make my earthly father angry enough to kill his own son?

There must be something wrong, either with the Quran, my dad, or both. Of course, I know now that my father is living in spiritual blindness, in slavery to the world and to the wicked one, through an evil spirit of false religion (2 Cor 4:4; Eph 2:1-3). To this day, I pray for my dear father's soul, that he would be redeemed, and that his eyes would be opened by Jesus.

Before I had access to the internet, I would feed my soul by trying to remember as many verses as I could, and several came to my mind that I did not previously understand until my family had disowned me. The words of Jesus now made sense.

> Don't imagine that I came to bring peace to the earth! I came not to bring peace, but a sword. I have come to set a man against his father, a daughter against her mother, and a daughter-in-law against her mother-in-law. Your enemies will be right in your own household! If you love your father or mother more than you love me, you are not worthy of being mine; or if you love your son or daughter more than me, you are not worthy of being mine. If you refuse to take up your cross and follow me, you are not worthy of being mine. If you cling to your life, you will lose it; but if you give up your life for me, you will find it (Mt 10:34-39).

Was Jesus speaking only to his disciples or to someone 2000 years later as well? His words are not just for those who saw him in the flesh, but also for those who would follow him in the centuries to come (Jn 17:20-22). Our Lord ordained his humble apostles to put in writing these words for all generations. He'd preserved these words, being all knowing and all wise, for me and others like me.

BAPTIZED

I had been reading in the Great Commission Jesus' words about the importance of confessing Christ publicly in baptism. About this time, I made a connection with some American missionaries residing in Bahrain, a small island off the eastern coast of Saudi in the Persian Gulf. I told them of my desire to be baptized, but they could not come to Saudi. I decided to take the ten-hour trip to Bahrain where I met these dear brothers. We celebrated my baptism under the cover of night to avoid government detection.

We walked through the hot sand to the warm water. Ten American brothers gathered around to witness my confession of Christ, two of whom joined me in the water and baptized me. As the salty water washed over me, I was reminded that, as Christians, we are the salt of the earth (Mt 5:13). I emerged from the water "raised… in newness of life" (Rom 6:4, ESV) and ready to follow my Lord wherever he leads me. What a joy it is to publicly confess and follow Christ!

THE BIBLE ONLINE

When I came back from Bahrain, I tried to find a Bible online, but all such websites were blocked. Then I discovered VPN (virtual private network), a way to create a tunnel underneath the radars of the government, hiding both location and identity. For the first time, I could read the Bible online with a secure connection, without fear of being discovered by religious police. What a hunger I had for God's Word! I couldn't stop reading it! Every spare moment I would read and meditate, feeling as though God had written the whole Bible just for me.

Time stopped when I opened the Word. Day and night blended together, and the Spirit of God filled my heart with joy beyond human description. Verses like "Give as freely as you have received" (Mt 10:8) moved me deeply, not simply to read God's Word, but to obey it as well. I could not sit silently. I had to share what was freely given to me by my Lord Jesus. While my fellow Saudi citizens were dead in their sins, I was now enjoying the true gift of eternal life. How could I leave them in the darkness when God's true light was shining in me? And what is that light? It is the message that there is no other way to the Father except through Jesus. A Muslim can do no work or deed worthy to buy redemption from God, and no ocean of good works can wash away even one sin. Like all mankind, a Muslim is helpless to reconcile himself to God. Jesus said, "I am the way, the truth, and the life. No one can come to the Father except through me" (Jn 14:6). Jesus, the true Isa, is the perfect Lamb who takes away the sins of the world (Jn 1:29). Now that I was saved and filled with this glorious truth, God was telling me to share it. It was my highest honor to obey.

AN EVANGELISTIC WEBSITE TO SAUDI MUSLIMS

Christ's love compelled me to start a chat room which I called "Jesus for Saudi Arabia." For the first time in the history of my country, there was a place for Arabian people to learn online about Jesus from a citizen of Saudi Arabia. No one could believe there was an actual Saudi Christian administrating it—they thought for sure I must have been from Iraq, Iran, Jordan, Egypt, or somewhere else. Sadly, because of this doubt, I was eventually reported to the host, Paltalk, a Jewish company. They blocked me, removed my access, and deleted my account. A generous Jewish-American Christian woman would later donate funds to reopen the chatroom, but we would be shut down again.

This, however, did not discourage or stop me from sharing my faith with Muslims! I knew they were blinded by Satan, able to see only according to this world, trapped in the deep darkness of their sin. "We are not fighting against flesh-and-blood enemies, but against evil rulers and authorities of the unseen world, against mighty powers in this dark world, and against evil spirits in the heavenly places" (Eph 6:12).

God has called me to preach the Gospel to every person I can reach (Mk 16:15). The Quran has enslaved so many people with its lies. It presents an upside-down image of the truth and describes Isa (Jesus) as a mere man. But I now know that Jesus is the divine Son of God (Col 1:15) who died for my sins.

With the truth now in my heart, I could not be selfish with the Gospel message. So, I went online again where I came across a Saudi believer seeking asylum overseas. We set up our own website, careful to keep it out of the government's eye. After a few weeks, however, we learned that the Saudi government knew about the website. Local newspapers even began to write about it, warning that we were young deceivers. Many denunciations descended from the highest authorities in the Saudi Kingdom, even from the Grand Mufti himself. Consider this snippet from a Saudi magazine article written about us at the time:

> The Grand Mufti of Saudi Arabia emphasized that the so-called Saudi Christians Organization is in no way related to the Saudi society and it does not represent it in any way. Upon his participation in a missionary meeting, the Mufti said that this group will not have any influence on the Saudi society, considering that the website launched in the name of this organization are but attempts to break through the Saudi

society. The Saudi Communications and Information Technology Commission had blocked the website of the Christianization organization called the "Saudi Christians Organization", and many local news reports in the past few days discussed the work of this organization, warning against its attempt to infiltrate the Saudi society.

With such high-level exposure, the Saudi Arabian government permanently blocked our website. Despite this setback, I continued to share my faith with the Muslim people around me via social media, especially seeking fellow Saudi citizens, as they have no access to the Bible whatsoever.

THE FIRST PERSON I BAPTIZED

Before the authorities shut down the Paltalk chatroom, I had the privilege of watching the conversion of a man and his growth into a serious disciple of Jesus. One day, while ministering in the chatroom, a young lady joined. She quickly became critical of the message of the Gospel and left abruptly, terribly upset. Periodically over the next few weeks, she returned only to curse and shame us, and each time, I would show her the kindness of Jesus. She then disappeared for quite a while, and during that time I prayed for her. You can imagine my surprise and joy the day she came back and informed us that she was reading the Bible and seeking the Lord to save her! The Spirit of God had lifted the thick, dark curtain of blindness from her eyes, and she now could see and recognize Jesus as her Lord and God.

Her cup overflowing, she desired to share her conversion with her uncle. They arranged a private meeting, and she took the chance to share the love and hope of Jesus. Her uncle, however, responded by mocking her, pointing at the Bible on her computer screen and saying, "What are the names of these books in the Bible? Malachi? Ezekiel? Nehemiah? These are strange names!" (The names in the Bible are translated poorly in some Arabic translations).

She was deeply hurt by her uncle's response. The uncommon kindness she had always received from him had transformed into scorn and mockery; yet, she returned home and prayed for him.

Her uncle would be unable to sleep that night. The verses she had shared with him echoed in his head. After tossing and turning for hours, he leaped out of bed, leaving a tangled mess of blankets in his wake and marched to his computer, thinking, "What if my niece is right?"

He was not merely curious; this was divine prompting from a God who loved him.

Searching his computer, he opened the VPN and began reading the New Testament Scriptures, drawn by Jesus' words which were unlike anything he'd ever heard. He then began comparing the Christian Scriptures with the Quran. As he weighed the two, the words of Jesus touched his heart in ways and in depths not a single word in the Quran had ever done. These were sweet and inviting words of pure love!

After a rich study of the New Testament, testing the Quran thoroughly against the Bible, he found his comfort in the words of Jesus and surrendered his life and eternity to his new Lord and Savior, Jesus Christ!

The next day he told me in our chatroom of his conversion and expressed his desire to be baptized. I left immediately to meet him at his home. It was a long but burdenless journey, for a hard man had been turned to moldable clay by the love of Christ. When I arrived in his town, he welcomed me. It was our first face-to-face contact. What a miracle that two men raised in Islam were now following Jesus the Messiah! I entered his home, and he showed me where he had prepared a bathtub for his baptism.

Before proceeding, we sat together and drank tea while we studied the Scriptural meaning of baptism: a symbol of death to one's old life and a spiritual resurrection in new birth. He agreed joyfully with God's Word, and together we waded into the waters of baptism. This was my first time following God's command to make disciples: "baptizing them in the name of the Father and of the Son and of the Holy Spirit" (Mt 28:19). We tried our best to follow the model of our Lord, who himself was baptized in the Jordan River. Though no river, our God had provided a bathtub, and that was more than enough.

As he knelt in the narrow vessel, I said to him, "In obedience to Jesus' command, I baptize you in the name of the Father and the Son and the Holy Spirit."

This was the beginning of a strong brotherhood between a former Sunni Muslim (me) and a former Shiite Muslim (my new friend). Alienated by fourteen hundred years of war and a divided doctrine of hatred and destruction, we were brought together in the love of Christ. "For Christ himself has brought peace to us. He united Jews and Gentiles into one people when, in his own body on the cross, he broke down the wall of hostility that separated us" (Eph 2:14).

A TRIP TO SEE MY SPIRITUAL FATHER

The next year, during a short break from school, I decided to go back to Auckland, New Zealand, to see my father in the faith. What a joy it was to be discipled by him in the Word of God! Each day we spent time reading and studying the Bible together, and I was invited to speak in churches around New

Zealand. This was my first time publicly testifying of my conversion and surrender to Christ. People were astounded and praised God for all he had done in my life. My father in the faith was there with me every step of the way.

We went to Marsden Cross in New Zealand, the very place on that island where it is said that the Gospel was first preached. New Zealand is literally at the end of the earth, the last piece of land before Antarctica. I remember thinking, "Jesus commanded the Gospel to be preached to the very ends of the earth—and here I am at the end of the earth!"

On the last day of my trip, while meditating on the Scripture, I read a passage in which Jesus commands his apostles to preach the Gospel and take nothing with them.

> Then he sent them out to tell everyone about the Kingdom of God and to heal the sick. "Take nothing for your journey," he instructed them. "Don't take a walking stick, a traveler's bag, food, money, or even a change of clothes. Wherever you go, stay in the same house until you leave town. And if a town refuses to welcome you, shake its dust from your feet as you leave to show that you have abandoned those people to their fate." So they began their circuit of the villages, preaching the Good News and healing the sick (Lk 9:2-6).

Jesus was speaking to me personally, for I had the same burden in my heart. As a symbol of obedience to Christ, I gave my luggage to my spiritual father and departed for Saudi Arabia, taking only the clothes on my back and the sandals on my feet. Years later, God reminded me of his faithfulness when this same luggage was returned to me at my new home in America.

A CHRISTIAN PILGRIMAGE TO MECCA

The next semester, I resumed my medical studies at the university while continuing to learn about my Lord. Each day I looked forward to getting deep into the Word of God. I was especially touched by David Platt's series on "Secret Church," described on his website:

> Secret Church is our version of 'house church' where we meet periodically for an intense time of Bible study—lasting 6+ hours—including a time of prayer for our brothers and sisters across the globe who are facing persecution and for those who still have not heard the Gospel.[12]

Because of this study, I one day felt moved to do something beyond praying for my nation. I read in the Psalms: "I will thank you, LORD, among all the people. I will sing your praises among the nations" (Psa 108:3). In Saudi Arabia, there is severe Christian persecution. "How then," I wondered, "can I praise Christ's name among the nations?"

As my studies came to a close that summer, I decided to go on a pilgrimage to Mecca, doing so this time, however, in the name of Jesus. I found myself surrounded by roughly three million people, both young and old, and all Muslims—except for one: me. I interceded for this diverse collection of tongues and tribes. I prayed day and night that they would know Jesus Christ, the one before whom every knee would bow and every tongue confess that he is Almighty God (Phil 2:9-11). I prayed that they would join us in the New Jerusalem as citizens of heaven.

Jesus said he is going to prepare a place for us in a city so enormous (1400 miles by 1400 miles) that it could cover the whole United States of America, Mexico, and part of Canada

---

[12] For more info visit http://www.radical.net/secret-church/.

(Rev 21:16)! Such a vast, eternal city awaits an incalculable number of people; there is indeed room for my Muslim kindred. And this is why I went to Mecca: to stand among three million people and tell them about the true God.

The Scriptures promise that if you seek the Lord with all of your heart, you will find him (Jer 29:13). Pilgrims in Mecca often pay a lot of money to make the trek, sometimes forfeiting their entire life's savings. For ten days, I blessed the masses in Jesus' name and shared the Gospel, engaging in many conversations and wading through a great deal of rejection.

PROVING THE QURAN WRONG

Why was my Christian pilgrimage so significant? Muslims believe that anyone who comes to Mecca's grand sanctuary cannot pray in any name other than Allah's, or they will be torn to pieces and brought down to hellfire by the demonic birds of hell.

In the grand sanctuary, there is a black house called the Kaaba, the holiest mosque in the holiest city of Islam considered by Muslims to be the *bayt Allāh*, the "House of God". It holds a role similar to the Tabernacle and the Holy of Holies in Judaism. Wherever they are in the world, Muslims are expected to face the Kaaba when performing *salat* (prayer); the direction they face is called the *qibla*. The Kaaba is considered by Muslims to be at the center of the world, with the Gate of Heaven directly above, making it the location where the sacred world intersects with the profane.

The Quran is clear that anyone who comes to this "gateway to heaven" and prays in any other name besides Allah will be devoured by demons from hell (Quran 105, 22:25). Quran

105 refers to the well-known event that supposedly happened in the birth year of the prophet Muhammad wherein Allah protected the Kaaba against the attack of a pagan army that, riding on the backs of elephants, came from Yemen intent on destroying it. Instead, it is said that Allah obliterated the great army, calling tiny birds from hell that pelted them with small stones of petrified clay. Allah will do the same, it concludes, to anyone who would defile the holy Kaaba sanctuary with a name besides his own.

Yet, there I was, praying in the name of Jesus from early morning to late at night, amid three million Muslims. I defiled the holy sanctuary with my prayers to the Living God, beseeching him to have mercy on every lost soul praying around me, to soften their hearts that they would come to the true God through his Son Jesus Christ! A record of my praying was even posted to social media for all eyes and ears to see and hear.

According to the texts on which I was raised, I had greatly offended Allah; but I was not devoured by tiny demonic birds. I lifted high the name of the true King and God Jesus Christ among the millions of lost Muslim souls, and no harm befell me whatsoever.

My Christian pilgrimage disproves the Quran's teachings. I stand in the truth written down by the apostle John who said: "Little children, you are from God and have overcome them, for he who is in you is greater than he who is in the world" (1 Jn 4:4, ESV). My prayer is that Muslims everywhere would be overcome by the love of Jesus and be granted eternal life because of his atoning sacrifice for all our sins.

While still in Mecca, I asked two American Christian friends from a well-known church to join me in prayer for the nations, and we set up a live Skype feed to join me in prayer for the multitudes there in Jesus' name.

I knew Satan would attack; it was only a matter of when. This is intense spiritual warfare, and I knew I was stepping onto one of the deepest, darkest battlefields, marching directly into the stronghold of a satanic powerhouse. I was not afraid to enter Satan's territory and there proclaim the power of the true Isa. In the following days, hell itself seemed to have opened up, launching an all-out assault of spiritual fire and brimstone on my life and the lives of those who'd joined my quest.

5 | TORTURED FOR CHRIST

*Bless those who persecute you.
Don't curse them; pray that God will bless them.*
ROMANS 12:14

I had no idea just how hard Satan would attack me. All territory belongs to the Lord: "The earth is the LORD's, and everything in it. The world and all its people belong to him" (Psa 24:1). Yet I know the wicked one has claimed this land as his own, and he will do whatever he can to be rid of those who proclaim the truth.

MUSLIM EVANGELISM

I resumed evangelizing online with Muslims. One of them, a Saudi citizen, seemed quite interested and asked many questions. We read the Bible online together, and I was always ready to give an answer with gentleness and reverence about the hope of Jesus living inside of me (1 Pet 3:15). Eventually, he asked if we could speak face-to-face instead of behind a screen. Showing my face to a non-Christian would be a huge risk; it could lead to my execution. But I knew that God had saved me through Jesus, and that Jesus is "not willing that any should perish" (2 Pet 3:8-10) but that "all should come to the knowledge of the truth" (1 Tim 2:4).

I gave no immediate answer, but I prayed for him as he had asked me to do. As I did so, I heard God's voice in the Bible: "Go and make disciples of all the nations" (Mt 28:19). The Lord was saying, "Go! What are you waiting for?" And in answer to my prayers, the Lord granted me peace, and I arranged to meet the man in a coffee shop.

During our meeting, the man inquired a great deal about the authenticity of the Bible. I answered patiently and gave him the truth of the real Isa with many sound answers from the Christian Bible.

"Jesus told us to love our enemies," I said.

"Muhammad loved his enemies as well," he replied.

"Killing your enemies is no way to love them," I told him. "How can you love them if you are willing to take their lives? Jesus killed no one but was instead crucified for our sins. He gave his own life for his enemies by dying for them."

The man answered, "When Muhammad returned to Mecca, he did not kill his own people."

"That's right," I said. "He did not kill the members of his tribe. Yet," I reminded him, "Muhammad killed many in Mecca who were outside of his tribe. He was glad to destroy anyone who had insulted him. Jesus, on the other hand, never killed anyone, but instead demonstrated his love to us in that while we were still sinners, he died for us. Moreover, he returned dead people to life in public resurrections."

I then showed him from the Bible how Jesus' work of redemption was observed by hundreds of eyewitnesses—not only his crucifixion, but also his resurrection (1 Cor 15:1-6).

"As he was writing this very letter (1 Corinthians)," I continued, "Paul encouraged the Corinthian believers to go and interview some of those same eyewitnesses. Muhammad's acts, on the other hand, were shrouded in mystery, with no witnesses. For instance, his ascension to heaven had no witnesses at all. The Quran speaks of this, saying Muhammad's ascension took place while everyone was asleep (Quran 17:1). Muhammad returned from his ascension and told his followers of his experience; yet, there was not one witness nor any evidence that any of that had actually happened."

Jesus' acts were almost always in front of witnesses. When Jesus was baptized, there was a visible manifestation of the Spirit as a dove, and the voice of God coming from heaven which all the people witnessed (Mt 3:13-17).

"God is holy," I continued, "and his justice cannot accept less than a full price for our sins. Our own attempts at righteousness cannot cleanse us from our unrighteousness; a payment greater than we can afford outside of a second, eternal death is required. The true Isa made that payment for us on the cross. Jesus is the Word of God and is the perfect representation of the Father. He is holy and perfect, and therefore, was sufficient to satisfy the justice of God for all our sins."

The man seemed to be receptive of Jesus as the way, the truth, and the life. He asked me to pray for him, and I, delighted, prayed earnestly in the name of Jesus that he would repent and put his full trust in Jesus for the salvation of his soul.

But what should have been a joyful moment suddenly turned chaotic as this man became furious that I had prayed in the name of Jesus. His rage was beyond comprehension, and I could see the anger cutting deep lines into his face. He shouted, "You are an accursed infidel! You are a pagan for praying in the name of a human being!"

He said much more than this, but my attention shifted to everyone staring at me in the coffee shop. As he continued to erupt, I lifted up a prayer for him, asking that God would have mercy on him and save his soul.

Such a man, I knew, could be angry enough to call the religious police.

I was right.

MY VIA DOLOROSA

I had barely made it back to my dorm when the religious police stormed through the door. Employing every ounce of their strength, they wielded clubs and fists filled with hatred and murderous intent, brutally beating my body into a broken, bruised, and bleeding pulp. Their clubs landed against my bones like blunt axes, and their hands carried fistfuls of lightning. They swung and clawed and kicked and smote, spilling my blood, teeth, and feral screams onto the floor. I truly believed I would meet my Jesus that day.

When at last the beating ceased, I was lifted from the ground; and there I saw a grisly pool of crimson in which lay fragments of thirteen of my teeth—these have since been replaced with prosthetics and dental restorations. I was handcuffed and chained like a beast with my neck, hands, and feet shackled together in chains. They carried me out, parading me before my fellow med students, humiliating me and treating me as a criminal—my "crime" being that I had loved others and had pointed them toward the loving arms of the Lord Jesus Christ.

My comfort came and still comes from the fact that, in my suffering, I was and am following in the steps of Jesus (1 Pet 2:21), who, carrying his cross, had also been paraded like a criminal on the Via Dolorosa (way of suffering). I can imagine what Jeremiah must have felt when he was forsaken by his own people. He even felt forsaken by God. "He shot his arrows deep into my heart. My own people laugh at me. All day long they sing their mocking songs. He has filled me with bitterness and given me a bitter cup of sorrow to drink. He has made me chew on gravel. He has rolled me in the dust. Peace has been stripped away, and I have forgotten what prosperity is" (Lam 3:13-17).

I was placed in a religious police car and taken away to a dark, dingy, and dirty cell. And so began an even more excruciating form of torture: mental torture. Day and night, they would blast the Quran into my confines—over and over, day and night, again and again, I'd hear the recorded chantings of Muhammad's message in Arabic. One such verse still echoes in my brain to this day: "Those who say that Jesus is God are infidels" (Quran 5:72)—over and over, again and again and again!

Surely, thought the religious police, it is impossible for the son of a mufti to be a believer in Jesus. I must have been overtaken by Satan or possessed by the "Yeshua" demon which could be exorcized through the ceaseless blaring of the Quran. But I wasn't possessed. I was awake from my sleep. I was alive from the grave. I had been born again by God's Spirit. And no beating could expel the love of Jesus from me;

no amount of brainwashing could erase the kindness Jesus had etched upon my soul. I now belonged to Jesus.

So great was my suffering in the days and nights to come that I longed to go home to heaven; it seemed like the torment would never end. Every day I would be beaten and put through excruciating physical torture. They would viciously whip my back and then rub salt in my wounds. They would hoist me in chains and beat my body and feet until I could no longer walk. Some days they would slowly drip salt onto my tender and bruised skin—oh, how it would burn! Torturing me was their daily delight, and they reveled in concocting new and barbaric methods to test on me.

I remained in religious solitary confinement 24/7, breaking only to be either tortured or interrogated. Under the blinding light of interrogation, they hit me from every angle, speaking of my family and reminding me that my father is a great leader in Mecca. I was told that a demon had possessed me, that I had gone astray and needed to return to Islam. But the greatest darkness and evil was shown in their ordering me to blaspheme Christ.

They ordered me to repeat: "Jesus is a donkey," or "Jesus is a dog," hour after hour as they laughed and mocked me; and if I refused, they would lash my back. Eventually I was whipped so many times that my back was ripped wide open. Once again, they violently rubbed salt into my wounds, shouting amid their maniacal laughter as their hands ran red with my blood, "Where is your Jesus? Let him come and save you!"

As the pain seared my flesh, I wished for a fire to fall from above and burn them off the face of the earth. You see how great a sinner I am? God sustained me by his grace, and I have since repented of my bitter thoughts. I should have loved my enemies, as I love them now, and pray that they will turn to Jesus. But this was suffering like I'd never known before—pain upon pain, without end; my body aching all the time without relief; my skin burning, head pounding; no rest; and no help from God. I felt forsaken and nearly fell into despair, but the Holy Spirit inside of me whispered encouragement with greater persistence than the whips of the wicked.

I was hated because they hated Jesus. What an honor to suffer for my Lord and King! The words of Jesus at last made sense to me: "God blesses you when people mock you and persecute you and lie about you and say all sorts of evil things against you because you are my followers. Be happy about it! Be very glad! For a great reward awaits you in heaven. And remember, the ancient prophets were persecuted in the same way" (Mt 5:11-12).

My struggle was not against human beings, but rather against spiritual beings, fallen angels (Eph 6:12-13), who had blinded the eyes of my tormentors. A few months before that time, I was in Mecca praising the name of the Lord Jesus Christ among the nations. But now the prince of darkness was stirred up, knowing his time is short (Mk 3:27; Rev 12:12).

MY DEPARTURE IS AT HAND

What was happening? My life had been turned upside down, but the Lord comforted me in my torment, and I am honored to have suffered for his sake. He brought to my mind verses from Ephesians 6. "Stand firm," I could hear my Lord saying. "Put on the whole armor of God!" I prayed, silently and sincerely, asking God to help me stand. Then one day, God answered my prayers.

My back had been torn to shreds, my body bruised, and nearly half of my teeth were missing. I truly believed I would soon be publically executed, beheaded, as had been the apostle Paul. But I didn't care; I just wanted to meet my Jesus. And as I waited for my time to come, I found that I could relate with Paul's reflection on his nearing execution: "I am now ready to be offered, and the time of my departure is at hand" (2 Tim 4:6, KJV).

At my religious hearing, the religious judge told me, "You are so young. You have been deceived."

By the mercy of the true and living God, they decided not to apply the apostasy law! Had they done so, I would have been sent to the capital city and executed. Instead, they sent me to an Islamic mind renewal (brainwashing) center. I went there and easily passed all their doctrinal tests of Islam, having known all the answers as I am officially recognized by my nation as someone who has memorized the Quran, word for word without error.

After almost three months of detention in the Islamic brainwashing center, I had answered every question so well that the director of the center released me and declared me "successfully rehabilitated."

They boast that they are the "pioneers in intellectual treatment." But I merely gave them answers from my mind; they could not reach my heart because "nothing can separate me from the love of Christ" (Rom 8:38-39). By God's grace, I kept a sound mind for Jesus throughout my detention. My brain had already been washed with the blood of Jesus! His words are indeed true:

> My sheep hear my voice, and I know them, and they follow me. I give them eternal life, and they will never perish, and

no one will snatch them out of my hand. My Father, who has given them to me, is greater than all, and no one is able to snatch them out of the Father's hand (Jn 10:27-29).

This was to have been my final semester of med school, but that semester was lost to confinement and torture, and I ended up failing two subjects.

While in torture, I thought, "Ok, Lord, if you want me to be a doctor, I'll do it; if not, I have faith that you will always provide for me and never abandon me."

What will I do when I return to medical school, I wondered? Will they allow me to finish?

6 | A FUTURE AND A HOPE

*"For I know the plans I have for you," says the Lord.
"They are plans for good and not for disaster,
to give you a future and a hope."*
JEREMIAH 29:11

I asked the dean of the college for mercy. I couldn't tell him the reason for my absence, but I pleaded with him and the medical directors to give me another chance. They had a meeting to discuss my case, and in so doing saw I had been an excellent student. There was yet hope.

A SCIENTIFIC BREAKTHROUGH

I was one of the few in my medical school whose research had been published in the U.S. National Institute of Science. Furthermore, I was the only one on a research team of accomplished international medical doctors, each with a stockpile of credentials and degrees to boot, who had not yet earned a degree. We had published research dealing with a possible cure for an autoimmune disease. Our medical trials had been performed using animals and was now shifting toward human trials. The dean said that because of my superior efforts which had resulted in the worldwide distribution of our scientific discoveries, the university would be willing to offer me another chance.

I was given one month to study for my final exams. I hit the books nearly seventeen hours a day. After a month of constant preparation and rigorous study, I sat for my exams and funneled all I had learned through my pencil. Two weeks later, I received an email informing me that I had passed. How quickly things change! A month prior, I had been a prisoner, chained and beaten. Now, I was a doctor. God is "able to accomplish infinitely more than we might ask or think" (Eph 3:20).

Upon graduating from medical school, one must apply for an internship as a junior doctor. Such jobs carry great responsibility and pay very well. It was imperative that I find a job quickly as graduates no longer received a student stipend from the government, and my free dorm contract was about to expire. However, since I had graduated later than everyone else, my peers had already secured their internships, leaving the pool of open positions looking like a barrel without fish.

The first hospital to which I applied was in the city. I had high hopes that I would be accepted into their program, but they turned me away saying, "Why are you even applying? The application deadline was weeks ago. How unprofessional you are to think you can stroll in here and expect a position."

Hospital after hospital, it was the same thing, "How can we trust you with the lives of our patients? If you have no responsibility when applying for an internship, how much less care will you have for patients? If we accept you, our hospital rating will be downgraded."

Dejected and unsure of what God was doing, I took a deep breath and looked to the very last hospital on my list. Upon my arrival, the Filipina director thoroughly lectured me, accusing me of being a lazy doctor. She was baffled that I had not applied months ago. I simply could not tell her that I had been delayed due to my having been tortured for believing in Jesus. But if I didn't find a job and quickly, I would soon be out on the streets begging for food.

My mind was swirling. Is this my payment for trusting in Christ? I prayed, "Lord, why would you do this to me?" I felt so alone and distant from the Lord. I even began to believe he had forgotten me. I thought, "What if I went and begged at a stoplight, and one of my brothers drove by in his Porsche, saw me, and rolled down the window to chastise and mock me saying, 'Look what your lord has done to you! Clearly Allah is punishing you, for you have gone astray!'"

The director continued lecturing, but my thoughts were so confused and my heart so heavy that I didn't hear a word she said.

A SIGN FROM GOD

When she had finished speaking, I rose from my chair and moved to make my exit, but I had become so overwhelmed with despair that I stumbled backwards onto the sofa at the back of her office. Burying my head in my hands, I squeezed my eyes shut and began to pray. As tears flowed freely down my face, I wept silently saying, "Jesus, you promised you will not leave us as orphans. Where are you? Everyone has left me, but I have faith that you will never leave me."

I couldn't stop crying, and when at last I opened my eyes, the room was all a blur. Wiping away the tears, my eyes slowly focused on a piece of paper taped to the wall above the director's head. I could barely make it out, but the inscription, without reference or attribution, read in English: "For I know the plans I have for you, plans to prosper you and not to harm you, plans to give you hope and a future."

My despair vanished, and I leaped for joy!

"This is Jeremiah 29:11!" I exclaimed.

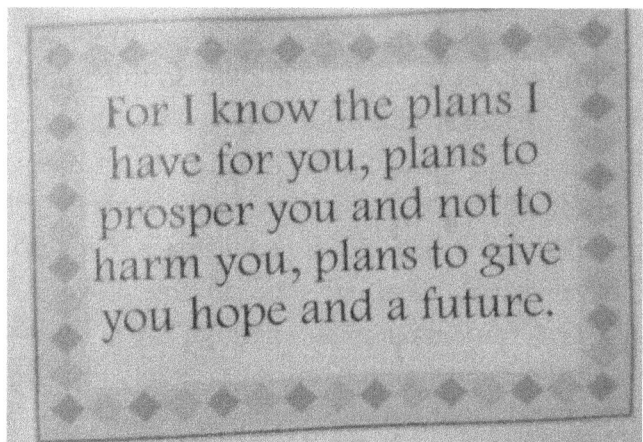

The actual sign above the director's desk

She became gravely frightened and jumping up from her chair, she began to shout at me, bombarding me with questions like a machine gun, one after another.

"Are you from the religious police?" she barked.

Given my long beard and Saudi clothing, she might have thought I had secretly come to interrogate her.

"No," I replied, lowering my voice in an attempt to calm her. "I'm just an intern hoping to work in your very respected hospital."

She eyed me carefully and asked, "Do you read the Bible?"

"Yes," I replied. "That is how I know the verse. But," I added, "you forgot to include 'thus says the Lord.'"

Looking me dead in the eye, she asked, "Are you a Christian?"

I didn't know what to say. Thoughts of jail, court, persecution, torture, and beheading suddenly burst into my mind. So vulnerable was I in that moment that it became difficult to form words clearly—additionally, because I had lost the structure of so many of my teeth at the hands of the religious police, I had been struggling to regain my speech. Now, in this tense moment, my mouth had forgotten all it had learned. How strange I must have looked to her, what with my misshapen teeth and labored speech.

"What should I say, Lord?" I prayed. "If she's a Muslim, I will surely be sent back to prison and probably have the rest of my teeth knocked out! But if I say, 'No, I don't follow Jesus,' I would be lying."

These words came to mind: "Be wise!" And then another verse: "I am a person of peace" (Lk 10:6, CSB). These were the very words that made up my reply.

"What is a person of peace?" she asked.

"Read your Bible," I replied.

She stared at me for quite some time, looking absolutely shocked. Then she took up my documents and said, "Give me your application."

I was dismissed, and we parted without another word. It would be an uneasy and uncertain next few days. All the while I prayed Jeremiah 29:11: "God give me a future and a hope."

This woman could harm me. She could turn me into the religious police. She could arrange for me to meet my Savior very soon. But to my amazement, I received a call from her one morning informing me that despite the lateness of my application, I had been officially accepted as an intern in their esteemed hospital. How suddenly everything had changed. It was a great surprise to me, but it was no surprise to God.

LIFE AS A JUNIOR DOCTOR

Working as a junior doctor in Saudi Arabia allowed me to finally become financially independent, and I rented a nice apartment in the city and purchased an SUV which was more than sufficient to get me around. I could not have been happier with this incredible blessing!

My days at the hospital kept me very busy. Shifts began at either six or seven in the morning and ended by four or five in the evening. Sometimes, I was on call for twenty-four hours. After donning my scrubs, I'd rush out for an entire day of seeing patients, reporting all my findings to the on-site senior doctor or consultant. In some situations, however, consulting the senior doctor was not necessary, and I would just make the diagnosis and prescription for the patient myself.

For me as a Christian, my workplace became my mission field. I prayed for each of my patients, but my favorite thing to do was talk about the Bible. Though I could not quote verses directly, I would preface what I shared with, "A wise man once said…" In so doing, I was being "as wise as a serpent and as harmless as a dove" (Mt 10:16).

When I returned home, I would read the Bible or share the Gospel online. But I really hungered for true Christian fellowship spanning beyond my own four walls and my computer. I just wanted to gather with my brothers and sisters in Christ, to share Bible verses and encouragement, or to simply lift up our voices together in song. Now that I had a vehicle, I had the freedom to explore Christian communities in Saudi Arabia and beyond.

7 | 13 HOURS TO CHURCH

Let us think of ways to motivate one another to acts of love and good works. And let us not neglect our meeting together, as some people do, but encourage one another, especially now that the day of his return is drawing near.
HEBREWS 10:23-25

There is not one church on Saudi Arabian soil. The only exceptions are the expatriates' churches at the U.S. and British embassies in Riyadh (not technically on Saudi soil). In fact, the goal of the Grand Mufti of Saudi Arabia is to rid the world of all churches. Ambitious though he is in this aim, the Lord says, "no weapon formed against you shall prosper" (Isa 54:17). I had great hopes that I might find a "forever family" in a local fellowship of Christians—this was my deep desire. To be healthy as Christians, we need to grow in grace through the fellowship of a local assembly.

HOME CHURCHES IN SAUDI

When I first came to Christ, I became hungry for good Christian fellowship, so I looked up nearby underground house churches and found several: Filipino, American, African, etc. These were comprised of foreigners living and working in Saudi Arabia. A typical group of believers would arrange a secret time to meet in an apartment, the walls of which would be draped with several layers of thick carpet to drown out the sound of singing, reading, and worship. A single peep overheard by the wrong ears could result in a raid by the religious police. In spite of the danger, the Bible commands us: "Let us not neglect our meeting together, as some people do, but encourage one another, especially now that the day of his return is drawing near" (Heb 10:25).

I was so excited the first time I found an underground fellowship. Finally, I would have a true family in Christ! Arriving at the meeting place, I knocked on the door; it opened just a crack, and into it popped the face of the leader of the group, a Filipino pastor. It was mutually understood that this was a dangerous situation, and I was prepared to answer any sort of security question he might pose. Perhaps he'd ask, "Do you love Jesus?" Or, "Do you want to worship the Lord? Do you want to know more about Jesus?"

I thought for sure they'd be open to a local Christian, maybe even overjoyed that someone like me would have any interest at all in Jesus. To my surprise, however, he asked me only one question, "Where are you from?"

Thinking that it would bring them joy to know God had truly saved a Saudi person, I smiled and said, "I am from here, a local."

My lips had not yet passed that last word when, to my shock and dismay, the door was suddenly and violently slammed shut. So hard was the pastor's swing that a substantial breeze slapped me across the face.

That was disappointing to say the least, but I was determined to find in my hometown my "forever family"—surely *those* Christians would accept me.

I found another underground Christian home group. Again, I knocked; but, to be honest, I was a bit uncertain. Like the other, the leader of this group, an Anglo American pastor, cracked open the door and asked me the same question, "Where are you from?"

Hesitantly but honestly, I replied, "I am Saudi Arabian."

Again the door slammed shut in my face.

Though I tried, I couldn't find a precedent anywhere in the Bible stating that if someone of a certain nationality tries to join your fellowship, you should slam the door in his face. A verse that encouraged me during this time references Jesus' words: "I have opened a door for you that no one can close" (Rev 3:8). I knew this was true. I just had to find that door.

Nevertheless, I was discouraged. God had saved my soul, but believers nearby saw me as a threat. Their fear was not beyond my understanding. I prayed that they would hand their fears to the Lord, and that he would show them who I really was.

Still, like Saul of Tarsus, I was to them a man who could not be trusted. "When Saul arrived in Jerusalem, he tried to meet with the believers, but they were all afraid of him. They did not believe he had truly become a believer!" (Acts 9:26). At least I was not alone. Saul's life brought me some comfort and respite from the persecution I began to face from every direction, even from professing Christians. I longed to find a group that believed the words of Jesus: "Everyone that the Father has given me will come to me, and I won't turn any of them away" (Jn 6:37, CEV).

CHURCH OF JESUS CHRIST

These home groups didn't want a person like me. It is illegal for them to receive any citizen of the Gulf States into their fellowship as all such citizens, governed by Sharia law, are forbidden to convert to Christianity. This is considered apostasy and is punishable by death. Nonetheless, I continued my search looking in places outside of Saudi Arabia since slightly more freedom exists in the other Gulf States.

I emailed churches in many surrounding nations. Each told me they didn't want problems and that I would not be welcomed. The only church that responded positively was called "The Church of Jesus Christ," which sounded like such a wonderful, inviting name. After encountering so much discouragement, seeing the name Jesus Christ made me so happy that I jumped from my chair and screamed, "My true people, the genuine people of Jesus Christ who will never slam the door shut in my face!"

After a twelve hour drive, I finally arrived. And there in front was a large sign with that beautiful name as well as a few small letters just below: LDS.

Upon meeting a member, I asked, "What's LDS?"

"Latter Day Saints," he replied.

Not sure what that meant, I decided to go inside where I met "Elder Eric," a young 18-year-old American, donning a suit and a golden name tag. I was so confused. His title was "Elder" yet he was so young—much younger than I!

As I conversed with him and others, I immediately realized something was wrong. They had "a form of godliness," but no power, zeal, or understanding of the Christ of the Bible (2 Tim 3:5). They were spiritually dead, and making a connection was impossible. Speaking with them further, I discovered that they believe radically different things than me. They greatly disliked my testimony and confession of faith in which I stated that Jesus is the only Son of God, second Person of the Trinity, and my Savior. Their faces were beet-red with anger before I had finished.

I thought to myself, "What did I say wrong?"

Maybe I hadn't spoken clearly enough, though I was confident that the Word of God on my lips was true.

When I returned home, I researched LDS and realized that they are a cult with a man-made book of religious fiction—a beginning eerily similar to Islam. The biblical truth about Jesus to which I testified had offended them, and now it was back to square one.

Will I ever find a place among a true church of God, I wondered, where I would be received and loved and able to serve Jesus? Would I ever find a "forever family?"

TOO DANGEROUS FOR CHURCH MEMBERSHIP

Still, even after all this confusion, I was determined to continue my search, and so I reached out to my brothers and sisters in Christ for help. A Dutch man—with whom I was in constant online fellowship, and who had previously come to see me (to ensure I was a real person)—contacted a "local" church on my behalf. They trusted him and sent me an email welcoming me to their fellowship. There it was at last: a "local" fellowship, though, it wasn't very local—I would have to drive thirteen hours each way and cross into another country.[13]

I was assured that the church would not mind any consequences of my attending, and that they were true believers

---

[13] To be specific, there were nine and a half hours of driving, one hour each way with stops for gas and food, and an hour and a half for inspection at the border.

and not another LDS group. The statement of faith on their website professed a belief in Jesus as God. Still, I wanted to be sure before I made the drive so I prayed until God gave me assurance.

Thirteen hours each way through the driest, most deserted, lifeless place on earth—this was my route. Thursday shifts at the hospital usually ended at five pm after which I would pack up and drive through the night.

When I arrived, the believers there would say, "How are you? How was the drive?"

Since I had just driven between the setting and rising suns, I would be so tired that I could manage only to say, "Coffee?"

I maintained this routine for quite a while. However, as time went on, I noticed something odd. After attending the membership classes, one delay after another prevented me from being received as a member. As part of the journey toward membership, one must meet with the elders. When I received my invitation and met with two of them, one was so moved by my testimony in Christ that he cried tears of joy while the other seemed suspicious of my faith's authenticity due to my having been pointed to Jesus through a dream.

I left that day with the understanding that the church would soon be voting on my membership. When the day finally arrived for the names of the membership candidates to be announced prior to voting, I was shocked to see that many who had been coming for as little as one month had been made eligible for membership while my name wasn't even up for consideration. I had attended for so long and had served in so many ways, yet I was considered unfit to join. Puzzled, I went in search for an answer.

Had they told me up front that they do not accept Gulf State nationals as members, I would have understood. Instead, they seemed to make excuses and even said they doubted my faith, despite the fact that I had been traveling this great distance each week just to worship our Lord with them and serve the Body of Christ.

The elder council had made the final decision. I was denied membership. Regardless of my admission of faith in Jesus, my belief in the Apostles' Creed and the fundamental truth that anyone who truly trusts in Jesus is my family, as well as countless reaffirmations thereof, I was told the decision would not be repealed. Thankfully the authenticity of my conversion does not depend on church membership.

This rejection in no way dampened my deep desire to become a member of a local church, for such is God's will. I bear no ill will toward those who rejected me. I forgive them and know that we are all weak and made of sinful flesh. And I must say that, despite this disappointment, the brothers and sisters with whom I served loved me and helped me to grow in my walk with Christ. Sadly, however, some of the leaders doubted my faith and still doubt me to this day. But my faith is grounded in Jesus Christ, not in man.

I say with Paul, "By the grace of God I am what I am, and his grace toward me was not in vain" (1 Cor 15:10, ESV). Also, "as for me, it matters very little how I might be evaluated by you or by any human authority. I don't even trust my own judgment on this point. My conscience is clear, but that doesn't prove I'm right. It is the Lord himself who will examine me and decide" (1 Cor 4:3-4). Paul's words later in the same chapter also give me great assurance:

> Our dedication to Christ makes us look like fools, but you claim to be so wise in Christ! We are weak, but you are so powerful! You are honored, but we are ridiculed. Even now we go hungry and thirsty, and we don't have enough clothes to keep warm. We are often beaten and have no home. We work wearily with our own hands to earn our living. We bless those who curse us. We are patient with those who abuse us. We appeal gently when evil things are said about us. Yet we are treated like the world's garbage, like everybody's trash—right up to the present moment (1 Cor 4:10-13).

I went on to attend other churches, to continue worshiping in obedience to the Scripture. None of the "above ground" churches could ever receive me as a member and retain their ability to meet publicly. Whenever I visited a church, I would often hear whispers of doubt about me.

They would say things like, "He's not a believer. He's the secret police investigating what we are doing."

This broke my heart. Here I was, a true believer from Mecca, but I could not be welcomed as a member of a Christian body!

Church after church, it was the same story: the moment I'd say I was a citizen of the Gulf States, people became very uncomfortable. I swallowed the bitter pill that there could be no membership in any public assembly in the Gulf States. I sought to worship at another church in the Gulf States but purposely did not seek membership or reveal where I was from so as to not cause any problems. My heart's only desire was to worship the Lord and be accountable to his people and his shepherds. And so I persevered, driving thirteen hours each way to worship and serve with God's people.

WEEKENDER CONFERENCE IN THE USA

Greatly concerned about my experiences in the Gulf Region churches, I decided to contact one of the leaders in the United States: Dr. Mark Dever, to whom some of the believers in my Gulf States church were connected. I took a two-week vacation and hopped on a plane, bound for America. This would be my first time in the country, and I was eager to see what American Christianity was like.

Landing at JFK airport, I took a bus to Washington D.C. where an American Christian brother from the Gulf States church would introduce me to Mark Dever. Originally, I had intended to fly all this way just to complain to Pastor Dever that my church in the Gulf States had treated me badly, doubting my faith and casting me away. I really wasn't concerned at all for myself, but I had to say something to prevent other saved Muslims from similar treatment. Having grown to love and respect Pastor Dever over the years for his powerful, God-anointed ministry and the spiritual food offered though his sermons, I felt confident he would listen to me.

When I arrived in D.C., I connected right away with my dear brother in Christ, Andrew. A retired Navy Seal from Louisiana, Andrew and I had met at a fellowship in the Gulf States when he'd tried to share the Gospel with me, thinking I was a Muslim interested in knowing Jesus. His genuine concern for the soul of a complete stranger greatly impacted me, and we've been dear friends ever since. He and I attended membership classes together, and it was he who would, without fail, be ready with some coffee after my thirteen hour drive. He has always stood by me and defended my faith—he is the definition of a servant and friend.

We arrived at Capitol Hill Baptist Church. It reminded me of the house with the white pillars in New Zealand where I first came to know Christ. Pastor Mark Dever's office was at the end of a long staircase. When we entered, we found him sitting behind his desk, listening to a Christian hymn and worshiping the Lord.

Smiling brightly, he rose from his desk and extended a hand to me saying, "You're the brother from Saudi!"

"Yes, I am."

"What are you doing in Washington, D.C.?"

"I came to see you."

He looked surprised and invited me to sit down. Doing so, I explained why I had come.

"Suffering is a part of the Christian life," he said when I had finished. "That shows your genuine faith." His words and manner showed his true empathy. "Would you be willing," he continued, "to speak to the 150 pastors gathered here?"

I was surprised! I hadn't expected that, but how could I pass up the opportunity to exalt Jesus in front of 150 pastors? I agreed without a second thought.

Time flashed forward, and I found myself standing behind a pulpit. Andrew sat before me among the pastors—not a pastor himself, but having a pastor's heart. Taking a deep breath through my nostrils, I parted my lips and out flowed my testimony and the story of my conversion.

"How can the lost believe on Christ unless they hear?" I asked the pastors. "How can they hear if no one is willing to go?" And with this, I put forth a challege, "Who is willing to go and share the Gospel in Saudi Arabia?"

I had the joy of attending the worship service at Capitol Hill Church the following day. Afterward, I returned to Pastor

Dever's office where he prayed for me and offered his final goodbyes. I would soon return to Saudi Arabia to continue laboring for Jesus' kingdom.

8 | PREACHING TO 22,000

Preaching the Good News is not something I can boast about. I am compelled by God to do it. How terrible for me if I didn't preach the Good News!
1 CORINTHIANS 9:16

My internship was a great success. After my short trip to America, I began serving as a full-fledged senior doctor, with my own office and secretary. I was now fully responsible for my patients and carried a greater workload, but this did not hamper my off-hours pursuit to reach lost people and encourage persecuted believers. As soon as my medical shift ended, the outside ministry shift began. A growing desire bloomed in my heart to obey the Lord's command to "Go into all the world and preach the Good News to everyone" (Mk 16:15), and I longed to travel outside my country and preach the Gospel and Christ's love to all nations. The only questions were how, when and where?

My first step was to take an unpaid, four-month leave of absence from my medical duties during which time I would get Christian training and learn how to evangelize more effectively. I had never taken the Word outside of my home country to share with others, but I was motivated by our Lord's words of warning: "Not everyone who says to me, 'Lord, Lord,' will enter the kingdom of heaven, but the one who does the will of my Father who is in heaven" (Mt 7:21).

I was and am willing to do anything my Father tells me to do and to go anywhere he tells me to go.

MY DESIRE FOR SEMINARY TRAINING

My next step was to enroll in a semester of seminary training in the U.S. I had previously taken some Bible courses through Gulf Theological Seminary, but they provided classes only two days per month—not enough to mold me into a sound evangelist. I did have the honor of being taught by one of their adjunct professors, Dr. Don Carson from Trinity Theological Seminary in Deerfield, Illinois.

I contacted the Southern Baptist Theological Seminary (SBTS) in the U.S., but I would need recommendations from pastors and be a member of a church to meet their requirements. Though good and godly requirements, they were impossible for me to meet having come from a place where Christian churches are outlawed. Forced to look elsewhere, I inquired at several other seminaries, but they all had the same requirements and could make no exception for me. After one final round of inquiries, the door for seminary training effectively closed. Nevertheless, I was not at all discouraged for I had learned to trust in the providence of my loving heavenly Father.

I turned my gaze toward service in evangelism ministries. However, after emailing a number of organizations, I found myself turned away for the same reasons as with the seminaries I inquired at. Worse still, I was met with suspicion and a

lack of love as they seemed unable to believe that a Saudi Arabian would want to know Christ and share the Gospel.

After a seemingly hopeless search, I was at last connected to a Pennsylvania operation called Youth With a Mission (YWAM) and ended up with one of their large coalitions in California. Many people in YWAM have differing theological points of view, but they have one thing in common: they love Jesus and want to spread his Gospel to all people. Together our passion was to obey Jesus' final command, given before he ascended into heaven: to share the Good News from one end of the earth to the other (Mt 28:18-20). How wonderful to see the different parts of the Body of Christ coming together to serve him (1 Cor 12)!

OPEN DOORS EVERYWHERE

My first ministry experience with YWAM was at a Vacation Bible School in Pennsylvania. On Saturdays, we would teach the Bible to children, and the rest of the week we'd share the Gospel in parks, schools, universities, the streets—just about everywhere. We traveled across the country to participate in Gospel outreaches and lift up the name of Jesus, taking the Word to Maryland, Virginia, Indiana, Kentucky, Arizona, Montana, and many other places.

I will never forget my first experience evangelizing with YWAM. Though I had spoken with people all around the world about Jesus through evangelistic video chat rooms, I was completely new to doing it face-to-face. Remember, if you do that where I come from, you get your head chopped off. We were sent out two by two (Mk 6:7), and because I was a novice open-air evangelist in a foreign land, my heart was pounding. In spite of my fear, however, I was determined to obey my Lord's command.

At first I hung back and let my partner knock on doors and do all the talking. I thought because he was an American, people would receive him more favorably than they would a foreigner. To my surprise, however, I consistently heard, "No thanks," and the door slamming over and over again. It reminded me of the slammed house church doors in Saudi, though some of these people were even less polite!

As I asked the Lord for courage, I realized that my partner was fulfilling a proverb spoken by the Savior: "Jesus himself had testified that a prophet has no honor in his own hometown" (Jn 4:44). In that moment, the Lord gave me great courage, and filled now with godly zeal, I waltzed forward and knocked on the next door.

What would happen?

I could hear footsteps drawing near. I was used to slammed doors, though I had grown no fonder of them with each slam.

Slowly, the door opened.

"I am here to share the love of Jesus Christ with you," I muttered with my Saudi accent.

"Where are you from?"

"Saudi Arabia," I replied.

"The country of oil! But, wait, you are not a Muslim?" they asked, greatly surprised. "I thought everyone from Saudi Arabia was a Muslim!"

"I am not a Muslim. I am a follower of Jesus Christ, and God has sent me all the way from Mecca, Saudi Arabia, to tell you of the love of Jesus."

Eager to hear more, the person invited me inside, and there I shared how Jesus had saved me. I testified about his love and grace to sinners and warned them to repent now and not turn away from Christ's love.

House after house the doors opened for me—not one slammed in my face. It had taken me 8,000 miles to find an open door of welcome, and here I was welcomed by unbelievers being drawn to salvation.

My final mission with YWAM was a large, several-week campaign to knock on 22,000 doors in California. I served with great joy and saw much fruit. People listened, they came to Christ, and we even held a baptism in which forty people publically confessed their faith in Christ.

SATANIC HARASSMENT

I was so delighted to finally be doing what God had called me to do. He has made me into an evangelist! When I speak about the love of Christ to the lost, I feel so alive, lifted by the Spirit of God. I am assured that I am fulfilling my purpose on this earth. But our common enemy has great power on this earth. "Stay alert! Watch out for your great enemy, the devil. He prowls around like a roaring lion, looking for someone to devour" (1 Pet 5:8).

The same satanic harassment I experienced in the Gulf States followed me to the U.S. Though unbelievers welcomed me to share the Gospel of Christ with them, some Chistians still doubted my faith.

One morning, before outreach began that day, I met with a YWAM leader who wanted to hear my testimony. For the sake of his privacy, he will be called Thomas.

"Tell me your testimony of salvation," said Thomas.

I told him of my life before Christ, of a time spent in deep darkness with no knowledge of the true Savior.

"I was not seeking after Christ," I said. "How could I? Bibles and churches are outlawed in my home country. But Jesus was seeking after me, a lost sheep."

Then I told Thomas how Jesus had appeared to me in a dream, and I joyfully confessed that Jesus had opened my eyes to His love and changed my life.

Abruptly, Thomas sprang from his seat and walked out of the room.

"What did I say to offend him?" I wondered, surprised and shocked. "Maybe he doesn't understand my Saudi accent. Maybe he'll come back."

But he didn't. He just left. So I went to the outreach and joyfully shared the love of Christ with hundreds of people, walking mile after mile under the burning sun, knocking on door after door, and speaking with person after lost person in the open air.

Later that day, I received a call from Douglas, my brother in Christ and leader of the Pennsylvania YWAM.

"What did you do?" he asked.

"What do you mean?" I replied, bemused. "I'm walking around, knocking on doors, bringing people to Jesus, and baptizing them in the name of the Father, Son and Holy Spirit."

"Thomas just called me," he said. "He's asking if you are a legit believer in Christ."

So disheartened and miserable was I at these words that I could offer no reply; words choked in my mouth. What more would men need to trust my faith? Are my actions not loud enough? I'd left my nice, climate-controlled office in a Saudi hospital to sweat beneath a blistering sun, with a backpack full of Bibles digging into my shoulders, nursing bruised knuckles from knocking on strangers' doors all day—I didn't even have my car! Those who had been lost believed me; they could see I had no other motive outside of Christ; and they wanted to follow my Savior. They could see it—why couldn't Christians?

I had to come to terms with the fact that some people would persist in their doubts about me. The Bible tells us: "There is no longer Jew or Gentile, slave or free, male and female. For you are all one in Christ Jesus. And now that you belong to Christ, you are the true children of Abraham. You are his heirs, and God's promise to Abraham belongs to you" (Gal 3:28-29). I am overjoyed by this, but may I add an extrapolation to this verse? There is neither Saudi nor American, but if you know Christ, we are all part of the same family and the same culture: the Jesus culture! Truly the "dividing wall of hostility" has been torn down (Eph 2:14)!

Many years later, Thomas would reach out to me and apologize. He asked also for a visa to Mecca, and I was glad to help him that he might share the Gospel of Jesus there and in the surrounding regions.

God worked mightily that summer. I went in not knowing what to expect, and the Lord gave me boldness and much fruit. So many doors were opened, and I enjoyed great liberty in telling people from so many nations and ethnicities about the true God who'd become man in order to save us all. God converted numerous lost souls, and I am still in contact with many of them to this day. Whenever I visit California, these precious believers still open their doors to me and show true hospitality, as they did recently, providing lodging and food and receiving me as part of God's forever family.

AN INDIAN FESTIVAL

While I was in California, our team was given the opportunity to evangelize at an Indian National Independence Day festival. When I arrived, I noticed some Hindu priests handing out their holy books. Drawn to them, I exchanged Bibles for their books and shared the Gospel with them. It was truly amazing and made me so happy to see them reading Scripture, some for the very first time. Just then, I spotted a distinguished gentleman wearing a t-shirt bearing Arabic letters. Sure that I was the only one present who could speak and read Arabic, I approached the man.

"Excuse me, sir," I said. "Your t-shirt says 'peace' in Arabic. But," I continued, "this is an Indian festival—shouldn't you be wearing something with Hindi writing?"

He looked at me crossly and very bluntly asked, "Who are you?"

Offering my name, I added, "I am a medical doctor from Saudi Arabia, and I have taken unpaid leave to come here and share the love of Jesus with everyone."

His eyes widened and he stared at me in disbelief.

"You are a liar," he growled, and then walked away.

I couldn't blame him. How often does one meet an evangelistic Christian from Saudi Arabia? Even still, I scratched my head, puzzling, "He doesn't even know me, yet he is sure I am not telling the truth."

Despite this strange conversation, I continued to share the Gospel and even saw some people give their lives to Christ.

As the day drew to a close, another man approached me and asked the same question. "Who are you," he said, "and where are you from?" I was becoming increasingly hesitant to answer this second question, but then he added, "Would you speak at my church tomorrow?"

The man in the Arabic t-shirt had told him about our conversation, and this man had since taken to watching me witness to people and pray with them in the name of Jesus. Though not at all expecting this turn, I wholeheartedly agreed.

I returned to my temporary abode: a cramped back room of a church building which I shared with the entire group. There I slept with butterflies in my stomach, so excited for this upcoming opportunity. And when the morning finally arrived, I waltzed with the other men to the garden hose out back, as we did every morning to clean ourselves in the open air with freezing water. But on this day I could hardly feel the chill. Sure, this was no ideal living situation, nor did I know what to expect this day or the next; but I was willing to do anything for the sake of the Gospel. "I have become all things to all people, that by all means I might save some. I do it all for the sake of the Gospel, that I may share with them in its blessings" (1 Cor 9:22-23).

The man picked me up on Sunday morning, and I stood before his congregation and shared my testimony of Christ's salvation. I was received by God's people with great joy, and to my surprise, the worship leader was the same man who'd worn the Arabic t-shirt!

After the worship service, he hastened to my side and said, "I am so sorry that I doubted your faith and called you a liar. Will you forgive me?"

"Of course," I replied eagerly. "You are my brother in Christ, and I love you."

"I could never have imagined a Saudi intellectual would come to know Jesus," he added. "I am a doctor as well, and a research professor at Stanford University College of Medicine. I have met so many doctors and intellectuals from Saudi, and they are so resistant. I thought this was impossible."

I smiled and said, "What is impossible with men is possible with God" (Lk 18:27).

Whenever I speak at churches, I always ask if anyone would like to travel to Saudi Arabia and partner with me in sharing the Gospel.

Most declare, "You must be crazy!"

Guilty as charged! And then, like Paul, I say, "If it seems we are crazy, it is to bring glory to God" (2 Cor 5:13).

To be an ambassador for Christ in this rebellious world is certainly viewed as foolish to those who have grown comfortable with their security in this evil age. At this particular church, however, the response was much different—it was downright enthusiastic! I met some people who were just as crazy for Jesus as I am! Some of them even rose to their feet upon hearing my question and shouted, "Yes! We want to see revival in Saudi Arabia! We will go!"

And they did go. A whole team of people signed up that day and applied for visas to Mecca! They actually traveled to Saudi Arabia and testified to Muslims about Jesus.

You may ask, "How is this possible?" While it is difficult to obtain visas to Saudi, I say once again, "What is impossible with man is possible with God" (Lk 18:27).

Not unlike Paul having Roman citizenship, an American visiting Saudi Arabia is granted privileges afforded to few other nations. Once all the hurdles of the application have been cleared, Americans are granted a five-year visa while most other travelers are granted a maximum of two years.

You may ask, "How can an American evangelize in Saudi Arabia?"

Under Sharia law in the Kingdom of Saudi Arabia, it is proper to ask a foreigner, "What is your faith?" And it is perfectly appropriate to answer that question in a manner that shares the love of Jesus. Surprisingly, none of this is a violation of Muslim Sharia law. A sincere question may be answered honestly without penalty, even if it is about one's religious faith. In this way, I have encouraged and helped many American evangelistic teams, and they have in turn successfully shared the Gospel with hundreds of lost Muslims and planted in their hearts the seed of Jesus' love.

You can imagine my joy when I returned to Saudi Arabia and saw my American friends in Mecca, sharing the good news with people in coffee shops, universities, parks, the city square, and in every other place a person could be found. Wherever there was an ear to hear, there they were sharing Jesus Christ. Such an effort has not been seen in Saudi for a thousand years!

During this time, my American friends visited me, and they beheld the fresh wounds from a recent attempt on my life, of which I will speak in the next chapter. These wounds testify that I bear in my body the marks of the Lord Jesus (Gal 6:17).

Seeing them, one of my friends took me aside and asked, "Ahmed, why don't you leave Saudi Arabia and seek asylum in the United States?"

"I must stay in Saudi Arabia as long as I can," I replied, "to share the Gospel and pray for my own people, for they have no other means to hear of Jesus' love and eternal life through him. If I don't go to my own people, who will?"

Paul's ambition had always been to share the Gospel where it had never been preached (Rom 15:20-21). I had already sought asylum in the Kingdom of God. My passport is stained by the blood of Jesus. I am a citizen of heaven (Phil 3:20)!

"This world is not my home," I told my friend. "God has made me a door, just like Jesus is our door to the Father's heart (Jn 10:9), and he uses me to open the way through visas by which Christ's flock can go and share the Gospel in places like Saudi."

Though I had become emboldened by Christ, I had no idea the suffering that was awaiting me upon my return home. That experience would call to mind the words of our Lord to the apostle Paul, "I will show him how much he must suffer for my name's sake" (Acts 9:16).

9 | LEFT FOR DEAD

I am the resurrection and the life. Anyone who believes in me will live, even after dying. Everyone who lives in me and believes in me will never ever die.
JOHN 11:25-26

When I returned to the Gulf States, I was eager to get involved again in the church. Longing to be in fellowship with believers in Christ, I drove to worship from Saudi Arabia to Dubai in my luxurious nine-seat SUV, reflecting on how joyful a time I'd had in the States and looking forward to worshiping with a multi-national church. From the moment I arrived, my cup was overflowing. What a joy it was to see my brothers and sisters in Christ and to hear the Word of the Lord preached with authority! The time of worship went far too quickly.

After a lovely fellowship, I decided to go directly home to Saudi Arabia, leaving from the church for the main highway, all the while mentally preparing myself for another thirteen-hour drive. This would be a tougher trip than usual for I hadn't slept a wink since the last trip the day before!

FACE IN THE DIRT

I left the city, my mind occupied with pleasant thoughts of the Lord, when suddenly they were violently interrupted. It all happened so fast. One moment, I was driving, and in the next, the four doors of my SUV had been ripped open, and a sea of hands came flooding in, taking me savagely by the lapels and throwing me to the ground with my face shoved in the dirt. It was the police.

After shackling my feet and handcuffing me, they took me to the Central Department of Criminal Investigation (CID) and placed me in a small room where they took my fingerprints, footprints, and a photo of my face. No one had yet explained my offense. I was in utter shock.

An officer questioned me, "Why are you coming almost every weekend to Dubai?"

Trying to be honest, yet wise, I answered, "I'm hanging out with my many friends. I'm also buying some goods from Dubai."

The officer had a long record spanning several years, documenting my entries and exits to and from Dubai.

"We have cameras everywhere," he hissed. "We know what you're doing."

"So, you know that I've been going to a Christian church?" I asked.

"Yes," he snapped. "And that's not allowed in Dubai because you are a Saudi citizen, and as such you are treated as a citizen of Dubai. The constitution criminalizes anyone who disbelieves in Islam. I don't think I need remind you that the punishment in the UAE (United Arab Emirates) is death by lethal injection."

The reality of the situation hit me like a freight train. I was completely at the mercy of my persecutors.

ESCAPE FROM DEATH

All through my interrogation, I could taste the scent of death lurking over my shoulder. I was soon escorted to a cell to be imprisoned once again for the name of my Lord. Perhaps now, I thought, I would meet Jesus.

As I sat in my cage, I wondered if my Christian friends in Dubai would visit me in jail. Did they even know I'd been arrested? The Bible says: "Continue to remember those in prison as if you were together with them in prison, and those who are mistreated as if you yourselves were suffering" (Heb 13:3). How I longed to see and touch the hands of my brothers and sisters with whom I had just worshiped, but no one came. No one had any idea I'd been incarcerated.

The intelligence officers must have uncovered my identity and learned that I had friends in different parts of the free world. Without risking protests on different continents, they couldn't detain me. So they came to my cell and said, "We are going to make a deal with you. Don't come back to Dubai, and we will deescalate this."

"OK," I replied, rather taken aback. Then, I asked what else would be entailed in this unexpected offer.

"Mark this document with your fingerprints," they said. "It states that you will not attend any suspicious meetings."

Not considering congregating with my brothers and sisters in Christ as a "suspicious meeting," I marked it as directed. But when I asked for a copy, they refused. So the moment they returned my phone to me, I quickly and secretly snapped pictures of my interrogators and whatever documents were yet in view to prove to the world that Dubai is free to everyone except its own citizens.

Upon my release, I drove immediately to see my Dutch friend and brother in Christ living in Dubai. The secret police followed and kept tabs on me the whole way; this my friend observed. I then returned home to Saudi Arabia and called one of the elders from the Dubai church to tell him I had been arrested.

He answered in disbelief, "So you are no longer coming to Dubai to worship?"

"Of course I'm coming back to Dubai!" I replied. "Do you think a piece of paper will stop me from worshiping Jesus? Not even the threat of death will stop me. I am immortal until God is finished with me!"

"When you arrive," he said, "we will conceal your presence and identity and bring you through a secret entrance."

It hadn't occurred to me that our conversation might have been tapped into by the government.

It had been.

AN ATTEMPT ON MY LIFE

The very next week, I jumped in my car and headed for Dubai to worship with my fellow Christians. A few miles before the UAE border, I saw a tanker truck parked in the middle of the road with its lights out. Looking back, I feel it had almost certainly been planted there by the secret police. Though I have no memory of it, I'm told I hit the tanker at full speed.

Miraculously, though my SUV was crushed to bits like a flimsy tin can, I emerged from my vehicle with only a few skin lacerations—no broken bones. I take comfort in King David's words: "The righteous person faces many troubles, but the Lord comes to the rescue each time. For the Lord protects the bones of the righteous; not one of them is broken" (Psa 34:19-20).

The cuts on my face, however, were quite serious. I am told that I had severed an artery and was bleeding so heavily that I may not have responded to CPR had the paramedics who'd found me arrived only a few minutes later than they had. Several units of blood had to be administered to save my life; and, in fact, the medical report states that I had gone into cardiac arrest.

My heart had stopped, but my task on this earth was not yet finished. "However, I consider my life worth nothing to me; my only aim is to finish the race and complete the task the Lord Jesus has given me—the task of testifying to the good news of God's grace" (Acts 20:24, NIV).

My SUV after the "accident"

RESURRECTION!

I arrived at the hospital in a coma, in which I remained for two weeks. When at last I opened my eyes, I saw only a jungle of tubes and machines connected to my body. It had once been me hooking up these machines and tubes to my severely injured patients; now I was the patient.

"What happened to me?" I wondered. "Why am I here in this hospital bed? I'm supposed to be at church, praising and worshiping my Savior! Yet here I am, half dead."

The nurse, noticing that I had opened my eyes, rushed to inform the doctors; they hurried to my bedside and said with surprise and joy, "Welcome back to life!"

I informed them that I was a doctor and asked what had happened to me. Having filled me in on the details, I asked to read my medical file. I had hundreds of stitches on my face, but I was not dead—I was alive and thankful to be so. More than this, I now bear marks on my face that show I belong to Jesus.

Those who hate Christ tried to kill me, and I will gladly suffer for him. "From now on let no one cause me trouble, for I bear on my body the marks of Jesus" (Gal 6:17). If anyone yet doubts me, let them look at my face. See these marks! The only reason they are here is that I belong to Jesus. Praise his precious and holy name!

While I was in a coma, I experienced a heavenly fellowship with the Lord, but I feel convicted by the Holy Spirit to not say much of it. Paul had a similar experience and testified: "I was caught up to paradise and heard things so astounding that they cannot be expressed in words, things no human is allowed to tell" (2 Cor 12:1-4). But I can testify to this: there is astonishing sweetness in the Lord's presence beyond anything I have tasted on this earth—a sweetness you wish would last forever. Indeed, I do wish that experience had never ended.

The Lord was merciful and used my time in the hospital to let me experience his love and prepare me for a deeper level of suffering that was about to come into my life.

10 | DISBARRED FROM MEDICINE

I once thought these things were valuable, but now I consider them worthless because of what Christ has done. Yes, everything else is worthless when compared with the infinite value of knowing Christ Jesus my Lord. For his sake I have discarded everything else, counting it all as garbage, so that I could gain Christ and become one with him. I no longer count on my own righteousness through obeying the law; rather, I become righteous through faith in Christ. For God's way of making us right with himself depends on faith.
PHILIPPIANS 3:7-9

Weeks after the attempt on my life, I was discharged and went to the police station to pick up my vehicle. Thinking I had arrived to steal spare parts, a police officer shouted, "Hey! What are you doing there?"

"Excuse me, officer," I said, calmly. "This is my car."

He looked at me. He looked at my crumpled SUV, bent and twisted there in the lot. Then he looked back at me with utter amazement in his eyes.

"What?" he muttered. "It's yours? You're alive? How could you have survived such an accident?"

I wanted to tell him I didn't think the cause of what he saw before him was an accident—but that was a story for another day. The SUV was unrecognizable. It did not look like an automobile, but rather a heap of tangled metal. Dried blood covered the interior looking as if a bucket of red paint had been thrown on it. Even I could hardly believe that this was my own blood.

A MUMMY IN A LAB COAT

After a few weeks in the ICU, I was discharged and returned to my work at the hospital. When my fellow doctors saw me, they reacted just as the police officer had; some looked convinced that they were seeing a ghost. That day, I was called to meet with the head of my department. I arrived in his office, wearing rolls of bandages around my face, looking very much like a mummy in a lab coat!

"What happened to you?" he asked, his eyes as wide as cue balls.

"I was in a terrible car crash."

"What kind of accident could do this?"

Pulling out my phone, I showed him the photos of my vehicle. What had at one time been a luxury SUV was now a heap of twisted metal.

Again, as had the police officer, he looked at me, then at the car, then at me again, before muttering, "You don't have any brain problems or breathing problems, do you? Nothing wrong with your speech?"

We physicians see so many tragedies, and I have witnessed some exceptionally horrible aftermaths of car crashes.

Even if a victim survives, they are most often crippled or trapped in a vegetative state for the rest of their lives.

My peers would tell me I had been incredibly lucky.

I believe otherwise.

BORN AGAIN!

"God has given you a new life!" cried my supervisor, speaking Arabic. "It's like you have been born again, recreated by God!"

These were the specific words he'd used—how shocking, I thought, to hear a devout Muslim saying such things, for these words are not in the Quran nor in Muslim theology or culture. How could it be that a Muslim would see that I am born again, but my Christian friends doubt my salvation? This man could say these words only if Jesus had put these visible marks upon my body! And it is my highest honor to bear these scars for him!

I couldn't help but testify for Jesus.

"I know who protected me." I began, "It was the true God. I was on my way to worship the true Messiah, Isa, when this happened."

The good news spilled from me like water from a fountain.

"No amount of good works can buy or purchase anything in heaven or undo our sin. God is holy," I explained, "and what is defiled cannot enter. Our sins must be covered by the One who is holy. Isa is the Word," I said, picking my words carefully so that he would understand, "and he is one with God. Isa died for sinners so that we could be forgiven and have eternal life!"

FACING THE LIONS

After moments of stunned silence spent staring at me, my supervisor shot to his feet and demanded I leave his presence. He did not appreciate my giving him the good news of Jesus and hastily reported me to the medical authorities. I immediately received a phone call from the general director's secretary telling me that my position at the hospital had been suspended. Later I would be called before the review board of the highest medical authority in the Kingdom of Saudi Arabia.

After many sessions of careful investigation spanning several months, they insisted the car crash had altered my brain and caused severe psychological damage. They offered to send me to a psychiatric center for treatment, but I told them, "My mind is perfectly sound. I have told my supervisor of my true faith in Jesus Christ. I am not ashamed of my Lord and Savior."

They looked at each other quizzically, wondering how they could best preserve my career and livelihood. Their motives were good.

Eventually they said, "Do you understand that this will cost you your entire career? You are breaking the code of ethics for healthcare practitioners in the Kingdom of Saudi Arabia. No Muslim can become a Christian. Such is apostasy. It is against the Sharia law."

I had kissed death and returned to life. Little did they know, I was longing to depart and be with my Savior. Death seemed sweet to me compared to this painful life; thus, my career meant less than nothing.

My answer, therefore, was simple: "Yes. I firmly stand by every word I said. I know what will happen, but I must tell you the truth and be honest. I must keep my integrity before the Lord (Psa 15:1-2)."

Squeezing me with financial and career threats had not prevailed, so they pleaded with me to consider my future wife and children.

In that moment I thought, "Who is my God? Is money my god? Or is my God the God of money who will provide for me according to his riches in glory by Christ Jesus? My God owns the cattle on a thousand hills! More than a thousand hills! He said, 'Do not worry about your provisions. Look at the birds and the flowers. Don't I provide for them? How much more will I provide for you? I gave my Son for you. How much more will I not freely give you all things?'" (Mt 6:25ff; Rom 8:32).

I was told to go home while they deliberated and that I would eventually hear of their decision.

EARTHLY "GRADUATION WITH HONORS"

After a few weeks, the final decision arrived. They called me in once again, and the secretary of the review board handed me their judgment. I read it. My position as a medical doctor had been terminated, and I was disbarred from practicing medicine anywhere in the Gulf States region.

I remember clearly bringing that paper directly to the shop to be framed, after which I proudly hung it on the wall in my room right next to my medical doctoral degree. From an earthly standpoint, I was weeping with Jeremiah: "I cry out, 'My splendor is gone! Everything I had hoped for from the Lord is lost!'" (Jer 3:19). But even more than the "achievement" of my medical degree, I see the loss of those very credentials as graduating with highest honors. All is rubbish compared to knowing Christ, therefore everything we lose as we press into knowing Christ is actually gain (Phil 3:7-8).

11 | REMEMBER SHILOH

Has this house, which is called by my name, become a den of robbers in your eyes? Behold, I myself have seen it, declares the Lord. Go now to my place that was in Shiloh, where I made my name dwell at first, and see what I did to it because of the evil of my people Israel.
JEREMIAH 7:11-12

I was no longer able to attend any church in Dubai. I'd lost my vehicle and my medical credentials, leaving me grounded in my city where no fellowship would accept me. Once again, I felt like Saul of Tarsus: I no longer belonged. But I knew Christ had saved me and that it was God's will for me to find and share in Christian fellowship. He would make a way.

Nicole[14], a born-again believer in Jesus Christ and head of security at the American Embassy, heard my story and, upon her request, had me added to the list of people approved and

---

[14] Name has been changed for security purposes.

welcomed onto the U.S. Embassy property on Fridays to attend a Christian fellowship. During the week, I would attend prayer nights and gatherings with both British and U.S. believers at their respective embassies. God had made a way for me to continue being transformed into Christ's image, and I was filled with joy each and every day because of it.

MY DOCTOR FRIEND FROM INDIA

The pain from the crash lingered. Smiling felt like having jumper cables attached to my cheeks, and I had great difficulty chewing food. The worst was a shard of glass resting on my facial nerve—who knew something so small could inflict such unspeakable pain? Four months I suffered in this manner, calling on many surgeons in numerous hospitals for relief, but none would even consider treating me as they were afraid they would cut my facial nerve and leave it paralyzed.

"Leave it there," they said, "and learn to live with the pain."

One day while at a worship service, a brother from India saw my pain and heard my cry to the Lord for healing.

"My name is Dr. Alexander," he said, coming up to me after the service. "I am a general surgeon consultant. The Lord has heard your prayers. Come to my clinic, and I will take whatever risk to free you from your pain."

All at once I began to rejoice! The Lord heard my prayer and answered so quickly! "Call to me and I will answer you and will tell you great and hidden things that you have not known" (Jer 33:3, ESV). God loves to surprise us!

Bright and early the next day, I arrived at the clinic and was promptly welcomed by my precious fellow physician and brother in Christ. We prayed together before surgery, then went together to the operating room. He assured me in Jesus' name that I would have no complications. Once again, as I lay on the operating table, he prayed over me in Jesus' name.

My lacerated face after the accident

He began the operation lifting praises to the Lord, and through his hands—and, perhaps, with the assistance of the Lord's angels—God worked a miracle. I was healed! There was absolutely no pain in my face whatsoever! He had removed the glass shard, and my face had not been paralyzed!

I was so elated that I could not form the words to thank the steward of the Lord's healing. But that joy was momentarily muted when I remembered that I was absolutely penniless. After my crash, the Saudi Arabian government had put a freeze on all my bank accounts, leaving me no funds to pay this dear doctor for his miraculous work. But God indeed sent to me a man after the heart of Christ, for Dr. Alexander paid for my surgery out of his own pocket—paid in full!

God is indeed good, but Satan is still the prince of this world; and for his act of kindness, my friend would later lose his job for having stood with me and acted in my time of need.

FREEDOM HALL

I continued attending the embassy fellowships until Nicole's redeployment to the States. The embassy grounds had become such familiar territory that I'd actually become friends with the guards and often volunteered to shuttle people from the embassy gates to the fellowship meeting place: a gymnasium called "Freedom Hall."

Front doors of the "Freedom Hall" where Christians gathered

When the new security officer arrived to take Nicole's place, it became instantly clear that he would not bestow on this Saudi believer the same friendly treatment to which I'd become rather accustomed. He sifted through all the papers, carefully reviewing his security measures and checking the list of people allowed on the embassy grounds. My name was second on that list. So shocked was he to see a Saudi citizen attending a Christian fellowship that he called the elders of the fellowship and informed them that I would no longer be allowed to attend.

"But he's a Christian!" they protested.

"It doesn't matter," was his cold reply. "He's a Saudi."

When the elders informed me, I told them, "Praise the Lord!"

Understandably frustrated with the situation, they asked, "Why do you say, 'Praise the Lord?' Aren't you hurt by this news?"

My reply was 1 Thessalonians 5:16-18: "Always be joyful. Never stop praying. Be thankful in all circumstances, for this is God's will for you who belong to Christ Jesus."

Though I was no longer welcome, I returned the following Friday, my trust in powers higher than heads of security, intending to worship with my Christian family. My friends, the guards, received me with a smile at the gates. They looked at the list carefully, hopefully, but then lifted their heads with sad expressions.

"I'm sorry," they said. "But your name has been removed from the list."

"I understand," I replied with a smile. "I just want to worship the Lord freely in the land of the free. I do have a U.S. visa," I continued, trying to persuade them. "And this is U.S. land, is it not? Let me worship with my Christian family."

Though it appeared to crush them, they had to turn me away. Of forty different nationalities in that fellowship, I had been the only believer of local blood—and that was the reason for my dismissal. Because this U.S. soil was located in Muslim territory, there could be no freedom for someone like me.

My search for fellowship eventually led me to an underground home group. The brothers and sisters there welcomed me, shepherded me, and cared for my soul. I finally felt at home. Charles, the leader and one of the group's elders, was like a father to me as was my precious Indian brother, Dr. Alexander, who also began attending.

During this time, I procured a very cheap and tiny Chinese-made vehicle with a manual transmission. Parking far from the home where we would meet, Charles would pick me up and take me to the Christian small group. Once again, God had paved a way.

SATAN'S INSIDE ATTACK ON THE CHURCHES

It had always seemed to me that in Saudi Arabia, the enemy would attack from the outside; never did I expect an attack to come from within Christ's church.

Some of the Christians in my home city had collected millions of dollars in donations from around the world and were very excited about the prospect of building the first permanent church building in Saudi Arabia. The secret police, however, keep a watchful eye on money like this due to international counter terrorism laws. If you deposit more than you earn in your bank account, you will be pulled in for questioning. For this reason, some of the Christians decided to secure all the money in a safe at a rented house. Perhaps you've already guessed what happened next: one day, the safe disappeared—gone without a trace, without an idea as to who might have been the thief and without a single shred of doubt in any mind that bringing the crime to the police would spell disaster.

The mystery, however, did not last long. One of my Christian brothers informed us that he had discovered a note, left behind by one of our group's pastors which read, "I'm sorry I stole the money. I needed it."

This man had made some disturbing appearances on television prior to this, speaking all kinds of prideful stuff. News that he had been the thief was, therefore and unfortunately, not very surprising. Man's true heart will eventually be exposed. This scandal was one such instance, and it led to further exposures from others when some professing Christians began making death threats. It would be a time of intense satanic backlash. But as discouraging as it was, it forced me to fix my eyes firmly on Christ. Even God's people may fail me, but Christ never will.

Though all these disturbing events were a surprise to me and many of my brothers, this was no surprise to God. Paul once told the Corinthian church: "There must be divisions among you so that you who have God's approval will be recognized" (1 Cor 11:19). I was praying that all sin would be exposed in the church of Jesus so that we might be a pure bride, ready for his coming.

REMEMBER SHILOH

Some people have asked me, "Doesn't this shake your faith?" It does not. My hope is not in men or in medicine but in Christ alone. He did not come to save the righteous, but rather to call sinners to repentance (Lk 5:32). None of this should be surprising, for God will always purify his own. Even in ancient days when God's people were drowning in their sin, he purified them at Shiloh, the capital city of Israel for 369 years during the time of Joshua and the judges. The people had taken God's powerful, manifest presence for granted. Leaders had become entitled and lazy. Amid the evil that grew by the day, God called Eli to repentance, along with his sons, Hophni and Phinehas, but they would not listen. God therefore sent the Philistines to burn down the Tabernacle. As the flames consumed it, Phinehas's wife gave birth to a son whom she named with her dying breath Ichabod, which means "the glory has departed" (1 Sam 4:21). The awesome glory cloud of God's presence then departed and would not return to dwell among Israel until Solomon's prayer at the inauguration of the Temple.

In Jeremiah 7:11-12, God asks, "Has this house, which is called by my name, become a den of robbers in your eyes? Behold, I myself have seen it, declares the Lord. Go now to my place that was in Shiloh, where I made my name dwell at first, and see what I did to it because of the evil of my people Israel." People fail. God never fails.

As the great hymn says: "My hope is built on nothing less than Jesus' blood and righteousness. I dare not trust the sweetest frame, but wholly lean on Jesus' name. On Christ, the solid rock, I stand; all other ground is sinking sand."

Christ promises to build his church, and pastoral corruption cannot thwart his design (Mt 7:21-23). Jesus said, "I will build my church, and the gates of hell shall not prevail against it" (Mt 16:18, ESV). I look not to men, corrupt and prone to weakness; rather, I set my eyes firmly upon my God and Savior Jesus Christ, unchanging and never failing.

12 | ALL NATIONS

My ambition has always been to preach the Good News where the name of Christ has never been heard, rather than where a church has already been started by someone else. I have been following the plan spoken of in the Scriptures, where it says, "Those who have never been told about him will see, and those who have never heard of him will understand."
ROMANS 15:20-21

Since receiving a new heart from the Lord, I have felt a great burden falling steadily upon me, pressing me to reach out to all the poor and abandoned believers in the world. Before losing my situation, my position as a medical professional had afforded me time off and a good salary, allowing me to travel to some of the most difficult and turbulent places around the world to encourage believers. During this time, I met many former Muslims who now followed and believed in Jesus as a result of online evangelistic and Christian chat rooms but told me they had since been forgotten. "Nobody cares about us," said some believers residing in two Arabian nations who opened their hearts to me when I made contact. "No one prays for us. No one wants to teach us the truth from the Scriptures.

We are abandoned and have no Christian community or fellowship."

"You are not forgotten," I replied. "I have been praying for you and would be overjoyed to teach the Word to you online. In fact, if no one comes offering encouragement for your faith, I will personally come to your country. If others in the church of God will not come to you, I will."

ARABIAN WORLD

I felt it was my duty to visit these precious believers living in Muslim nations. To protect their identities, I will not mention to which countries or cities specifically I traveled. My first trip was to an African Arabian nation. I flew into the capital of a neighboring country, then I rented a vehicle and drove ten hours to a border town on the coast—a most beautiful city! From there, I drove several more hours to the country's border where I waited an additional two hours while border security searched my car and reviewed my papers. Surprised that a Saudi would want to travel such a long distance to this African Arabian country by car, they asked, "What is your business here?"

"Visiting friends," I replied.

After declaring how much cash I had with me, I was released to make the eight-hour trek to the home of my persecuted brothers and sisters.

Using an encrypted web application, I made contact with the believers and was told where to go and how to arrive. I pulled up to a one-story structure, hardly worthy of the name "house". The roof was open, the floor made of sand, and bullet holes riddled the walls. I wondered if the roof had perhaps been destroyed by a rocket.

They served tea, and we all sat on the ground to pray, read the Bible, and cry out to the Lord for aid. I was there for only one day, but they were so encouraged by the visit, albeit incredibly surprised that I had actually come as I'd said I would.

My next stop was a city set at the end of a two-day drive across the worst roads imaginable, lost in the middle of an abandoned desert. There I met and stayed with two believers, teaching them so much of the Bible and quickly working through the Gospel of Matthew and John, doing it all in Arabic. This pair, out in the middle of nowhere, were not so far as to be out of God's reach, and both were so eager and responsive to know more about Jesus and his words. I stayed for a whole week in this forsaken part of the Arabian world, discipling my cherished brothers and worshiping God.

From there, I returned to my brothers in the capital city. We opened the Bible, prayed together, encouraged each other, and shared a meal. With eyes full of tears and hearts full of joy, we said our goodbyes, and I drove to the airport. To this day, I am in contact with these believers—oh, may our Lord Jesus open the eyes of multitudes among the desert peoples!

No sooner had I returned home when I learned of another group of believers in need. Residents of a Muslim country, they had heard through online Christian chat rooms about my trip to the African Arabian nation and reached out to me to ask if I would also visit them. Theirs is a radical Muslim land, known for being a hotbed for terrorism; but I felt the Lord calling me to put my faith in him, visit these persecuted believers, and carry out the Gospel by going to the places where God's people have been forgotten.

The hospital where I worked at the time allowed only one-week vacations; so, I worked some off-days and on-call days, in addition to my regular schedule, giving me more time off more frequently. With enough time finally saved, I flew to this capital city and terrorist training ground where I was met at the airport by my brothers. I quickly dressed in Saudi clothing and then was escorted to a car, everyone taking great care to ensure I would not be seen. We drove far from the capital city to a cave where we read and studied the Bible. We prayed for God's Spirit to move in our hearts as well as in the hearts of all believers in this nation. We read and slept and prayed for a whole week in this cave, divorced from the internet, phone service, and basic modern comforts, trusting in God for our sustenance and studying the teachings of Jesus. Each day I joyfully taught from the Gospels, answering my Christian brothers' many questions and revealing what the Word says about growing in Christ.

I could stay no longer than that week as I had to return to resume my medical duties. Before leaving, I emptied my bank account, exchanged it into their currency, and gave it to them—they were such poor believers.

"This is from the church of Jesus in Saudi Arabia," I said.

With one last goodbye, the brothers dropped me off at the airport, and I flew back to Saudi.

PHILIPPINES

Once I'd saved enough time for another week off, I flew to Manilla in the Philippines. After greeting me at the airport, my Christian brothers and sisters took me to a very nice hotel where they insisted on protecting me. Every night, one of the brothers would sleep in my room; they feared something might happen to me because I am Muslim turned Christian, and not a silent one at that. We hit the streets daily to proclaim Jesus' love; around every corner, I hoped to run into my dear Filipina housemaid, the woman who'd raised me so that I could share with her the good news of Jesus Christ.

One day, we met and shared the Gospel with a Catholic lady who was selling food on the side of the street next to a Catholic cathedral in the capital city. Wanting to offer me hospitality, she gave me a duck egg and invited me to eat it. In the Philippines, this is a delicacy called *ballut* which is a developing bird embryo (usually a duck) that is boiled and eaten from the shell. Its noisome odor was overwhelming. Its foul aroma nearly caused me to vomit, and my stomach pleaded with me not to eat it. However, in hopes that she would listen to the Gospel message if I accepted her gift, I slowly peeled back the shell, shut my eyes, and threw the contents against my tonsils. My throat quickly sealed, forbidding a wholesale swallow and forcing me to chew. As my teeth reluctantly ground, I could feel bones and feet crunching and even sensed a few feathers brushing against my tongue. I tried to think of happier things, but I could not help but see the physical manifestation of the stench, as well as a clear picture of what must have been going on in my mouth. It was truly a labor of love.

Delighted that a foreigner had received her generosity, the woman cheered and said, "Now you are a Filipino! You have passed the test!" She then expressed her desire to listen to what I had to say.

I began by telling her that I had been raised by a Filipina whom I loved as a mother. From there, I explained the meaning of Christ's death and resurrection. She asked many questions.

"What is the status of Mary in the Bible? Shouldn't she be worshiped since she is the mother of God?"

"No," I replied. "Mary is not a co-redeemer with Christ. Jesus is the only way to the Father."

I showed her in a Tagalog[15] Bible where Jesus asks:

> "Who is my mother? Who are my brothers?" Then he pointed to His disciples and said, "Look, these are my mother and brothers. Anyone who does the will of my Father in heaven is my brother and sister and mother!" (Mt 12:48-50).

Having planted a seed in her heart, I put her in contact with my Filipino Christian brothers that they might continue to supply the water of the Word.

We then traveled to the north side of the island to villages around Baler. There we shared the Gospel with many poor farmers who had never heard it before, many of whom believed in things like mysticism and evil spirits. Some would not listen and just walked away. Others cursed us and called upon spirits to attack and kill us. But there were a handful who wanted to hear more. These would later receive Christ as Savior, and we baptized them in the Baler Bay in the Philippine Sea. My Filipino brothers then guided them to a fellowship of Christians in the city.

I then hopped on an old, rickety airplane and flew to one of the southern islands, to the city of Cebu, where I spoke in two churches, one in the morning and the other in the afternoon. That night, I took another airplane to Mindanao, Philippines, where I shared the Gospel with many Muslims living there. They were not receptive in the least—some were even hostile—though all were certainly fascinated that a Christian had come from the birthplace of Islam. The Christians I met

---

[15] A Filipino language

there, on the other hand, were greatly encouraged for they had not believed that Muslims were capable of trusting in Jesus to be saved. I was living proof it could indeed happen.

As with the other weeks of my travels, the end came all too soon, and I flew back to Saudi Arabia.

CHINA

Several Chinese believers I met in the UAE asked me to join them and speak in China. I first flew to Hong Kong to meet a few believers, then to Beijing where I learned about the difference between state and true (underground) churches. I would later teach on sharing the Gospel with Muslims at some of these fellowships.

On one such occasion, we pulled up to a building that looked like a conference hall. I was expecting to see a gigantic cross shadowing the entrance, but there were no signs betraying this place as a church. Shortly upon entering, I was warmly welcomed and invited to teach. This would be the first time I would speak to a crowd with the help of an interpreter, something with which I struggled at first. Just as soon as I had a good thought going, I would have to wait for it to be interpreted. But God gave much grace and patience that he might offer these people his blessings.

Shanghai was next on the map where, in a Sunday service, I had the awesome privilege of witnessing literally tens of thousands of worshipers. So many were gathered that they were flooding out to the streets, all praising Jesus in their Chinese language and singing with all their might to God. I tried to join in with them as best I could even though I did not know very much Chinese. In fact, I understood nothing! But I knew they were praising my Lord Jesus Christ; so, how could I not at least attempt to sing with them? The preacher spoke the Word of God for about forty minutes. Again, I did not understand a word, but I was blessed to be among my brothers and sisters in Christ. The service ran from beginning to end without any problems. So, I wonder if there had also been Christian police in attendance as this was surely an illegal meeting.

I spent my last three days training my Chinese brothers and sisters how to evangelize Muslims and informing them of the beliefs of Islam. They needed to know the deep darkness of that religion and the desperate need of the Muslim people for Christ.

TO THE ENDS OF THE EARTH

Because of the generous salary I'd received as a doctor, I had the time and money needed to travel around the world and experience firsthand the multi-cultural church of Jesus Christ, all for one goal: advancing the kingdom of God in obedience to my Lord's great commission. It was and is still my burning desire to preach Christ, both nearby and to the farthest reaches of the world, spreading the Gospel of his forgiveness through his death on the cross and resurrection from the dead.

13 | BULLETS

Yes, and everyone who wants to live a godly life in Christ Jesus will suffer persecution.
2 TIMOTHY 3:12

After being disbarred from medicine, I spent many months without a job and only a small medical pension to sustain me. During that time, I witnessed day and night to many throughout the world on a video application, cheerfully giving the good news of Jesus. What a joy to obey Jesus' commandments, written by his hand and Holy Spirit into the very walls of my heart and mind!

Eventually, the Lord opened a door to the United States where I would once again go and proclaim the saving power of Christ at a couple of church meetings. The Lord moved in the people's hearts. They were amazed that God would save someone like me. As I have come to expect, they were initially suspicious, but after receiving my story in near totality, they could not deny that Jesus Christ had saved my soul. The Lord even connected me to my pastor in the United States. I experienced an abundance of love among my American brothers and sisters, but the time soon came for me to return to the

Kingdom of Saudi Arabia to start a ministry that would open the door for Christians around the world to come and evangelize in a place so desperately lost as my home.

My treasure in Christ could not be contained. I simply had to tell the world of my sweet Savior's love! Upon returning home, I resumed evangelism via the video app, reaching people of all sorts: Muslims, atheists, believers lost in sin—anyone who would listen! "He who has ears to hear, let him hear" (Mt 11:15).

It wasn't long, however, before I realized the Saudi government was tracking me. Unhappy about my Christian evangelism efforts and connections, they would soon pay me a visit.

CURSED INFIDEL

One day while running errands, I approached a speedbump at which time someone in a car to my left rolled down their window, pointed at my car, and began laughing at me.

Surprised and a little concerned, I rolled down my window and asked, "Are you ok?"

"You are a cursed infidel!" he screeched amid his swelling laughter.

"Excuse me?" I replied, taken aback. "Do I know you?"

Snickering, he pointed toward the rear of my car and said, "Look at your back window."

Immediately I stopped my car and walked around to the back. There, spray-painted across the glass were the words, "Cursed Infidel," as well as the infamous letter "N" (ن) scrawled in Arabic which is a symbol for "Follower of Jesus of Nazareth."

A chill fell over me, and I rushed back into my car to contact my pastor in the United States. Though I felt I should be saying my final goodbye, I asked him to pray for me, for I knew that I would now be hunted like an animal. Before doing anything else, I hastened to a repair shop and had the back window replaced.

A DISTURBING LETTER

I wasted no time in following Jesus' instruction from Matthew 10:23: "When you are persecuted in one town, flee to the next." A few days after moving out and settling into a new workcamp nearly three hours away, I found an envelope attached to my car. It was somewhat bulging and terribly heavy. I thought perhaps I'd parked in the wrong parking space, and someone was kindly notifying me. But it was so unusually weighty, I couldn't help feeling this had little to do with my parking. A fearful curiosity overtook me, and I carefully peeled back the seal. It was no friendly note. A flash of gold cut across my eyes, and with a trembling hand, I tipped the envelope toward my open palm. I gazed horrified at three bullets gleaming in my hand and offering a perfume of death. Hurling these into the dust, I extracted the envelope's final piece of content: a note, written in Arabic, offering a warning and a threat in this manner:

> *Dog of Jesus, you must stop speaking in the name of Jesus and turn to Allah and Muhammad his messenger. If you do not return to Islam, we will kill you. We are giving you ten days. You can run, but we will find you, hunt you down, and kill you.*

They would not wait ten days, this I knew. It was time to go on the run. Like a refugee, I fled to a Saudi work camp where I hid from these terrorists' gaze with little more than the bare minimum of food and water to keep me going. I traveled only at night to get supplies lest I fall into the hands of my hunters or the religious police. Days and nights sailed by this way in the concealment of my hiding place.

RAINING BULLETS

While out one night to purchase food, I saw out of the corner of my eye a mass of black rushing toward me. When I turned, I beheld a giant SUV and an assault rifle leaping out of its side window. I had been promised ten days, but I knew their thirst for me would be too great to deny for so long. Before I could react, a sound like popcorn kernels exploding in stereo filled my car as bullets rained down upon me. By God's grace, not one succeeded to penetrate my vehicle and find my flesh. After a perilous series of dangerous maneuvers through the city streets, I outran the terrorists and found safety. Never had I been more thankful for my little Chinese-made, manual transmission car.

Going back to the work camp was out of the question so I gathered a few odds and ends and began moving from town to town, constantly on the move. I prayed all that time for guidance and eventually felt impressed by the Lord that it was time to leave Saudi. I had almost no funds for a plane ticket, but the Lord put it on someone's heart to provide almost the exact provision in my bank account necessary for my airline passage.

I got in my little car and set a course for the Dubai airport in the United Arab Emirates. It was a long and sandy road, and it should have been remote enough to avoid detection. But I soon heard the roar of that giant SUV rumbling toward me at full speed, a cloud dust in its wake, determined to assassinate me.

As quickly as a shark speeding toward the kill, the SUV was on top of me, and a barrage of bullets blasted through my windows and doors, erupting with such force that I felt my bones had all been pulverized. For over thirty minutes, I raced about the barren landscape trying to elude my predators; every second was an eternity, and every breath felt sure to be my last. Steaming shards of lead whizzed past my face and exploded all around me. I jerked the wheel this way and that, trying to navigate the pitch dark ahead of me when all of a sudden, what felt like a searing knife stabbed me in my shoulder. I quickly glanced at my wound but could see nothing in this darkness. Just that moment another bullet sailed through my dashboard. Any pain I felt from the bullet that had just seared me was forgotten.

I drove like a madman but could not shake them. It seemed I would be running in this manner until I finally ran out of gas. But then, as if I'd run over a landmine, my car jolted, bounced, and began to spin violently. "This is the end," I thought as the wheel whirled out of my hands and I lost all control. "I'm going to graduate and meet Jesus!"

Just then, I slammed into a sand dune. Unsure whether I was dead or alive, I whipped open the car door and ran as fast as I could into the Arabian desert. Sand and hot winds coated and dried my throat, but this was a mad dash for survival. Each breath felt increasingly like my lungs were trying to lift an ever-growing bowling ball. They became so fatigued, they felt flat, unable to draw air.

Outside of my will, I collapsed face-first into the sand awaiting my death at any moment. Surely the terrorists must be closing in on me.

"Lord," I prayed, "you said flee, and I fled! I'll soon see you face-to-face! How I long for that sweet fellowship!"

Eternity passed, and still no one came to kill me. Having regained my breathing and summoning enough strength to stand, I returned to my car buried in the sand dune; but, to my utter amazement, no one was around. Did they think they'd killed me and just drove off? I would not ponder this question for long. If it was not yet my time to meet Jesus, if Christ had yet some plan for my life, then there would still be more running ahead. So I started digging my car out.

ALIVE FROM THE DEAD

By God's grace, I freed my car from the sand dune. Hobbling down the highway in my chewed-up car, I wasn't sure if I was dead or alive. Could I really be alive? I could hardly believe it! As I approached the border, I prayed and asked God for wisdom. A car riddled with bullets would surely raise suspicion.

DUCT TAPE SAVED THE DAY

Before approaching the border, I stopped at a local supermarket for food and water. I was absolutely drained from the recent event. As I walked the aisles, praying all the while, my eyes fell on some duct tape. For a minute, it seemed misplaced, but then I realized that this was the answer to my prayer! The tape, to my joyful astonishment, matched the color of my car exactly! This was such a quick and clear answer to prayer that I feel like I had just missed seeing an angel place it there for me to find!

Purchasing the tape, I proceeded to cover all the bullet holes—what a perfect match! Using my elbows, I smashed out what remained of my shattered windows, leaving gaping holes that I would later tape over to avoid the sand, heat, and humidity. I then continued toward Dubai. Miraculously, and thanks to the earnest prayers from my friends in New Zealand and the U.S., I passed through the border without issue.

My duct taped car, hiding the bullet holes and bullet strewn window

Before going to the airport, I visited a friend with whom I prayed and shared a delicious meal. His wife entered their house in shock. Looking at me with wide eyes, she said, "Your car is completely wrecked! Things are hanging from the bottom! It's undriveable!"

I told them the whole story, and afterward my dear friend went out with me to the car to examine the bullet holes and the smashed windows. As we did so, I discovered a bullet lodged in the driver's seat, stopping just shy of penetrating the fabric in the exact location where my heart had been. It is very possible I had been pursued by a professional sniper, for who can shoot with this precision from a moving car at night? But all the greatest marksmen in the world could not prevail against my witness protection program which is the strongest in all the universe; for I witness for the sake of the Gospel, and the Lord God protects me.

Just then, I remembered the searing knife that had stabbed me in the dark. When I looked, I found a crimson shoulder, still bleeding, with a bullet fragment lodged beneath my skin.

My friend helped me patch myself up. Then we prayed, and I left for the Dubai airport. I asked God for a place to hide my car, and he showed me the perfect spot: a mechanic's garage just next to the airport. My car blended in perfectly with all the other damaged cars!

A NARROW ESCAPE

When I arrived at the airport, there was a long queue of people waiting for their boarding passes. I thought for sure I would miss my flight. Just then someone shouted, "Anyone going to Auckland, New Zealand?"

"I am!" I shouted back.

I was approached by a man who took me past the crowd to the immigration line where I was quickly issued a boarding pass. Citizens of the Gulf States, unlike those of any other nation, are permitted to pass directly through security using a Gulf States identification card. I had used different forms of

ID when exiting the UAE than when I'd entered, making my coming and going untraceable this time.

As soon as I got onto the airplane, I heaved a deep sigh of relief! However, that relief would be short-lived, for upon my arrival in New Zealand, I received bad news that three of my foreign friends had been arrested and interrogated, some of them for several days. Additionally, I was informed that I had indeed barely escaped. Only minutes after my departure, the police swarmed my gate looking for me. Upon realizing they had missed me, they immediately went after my friends and fellow believers. Hearing that others had been persecuted because of me was unbearable. Thankfully, they were all later released without charge.

My fifteen-hour flight to New Zealand felt like fifteen minutes. At last I was free—I was finally safe.

Or so I thought.

14 | ESCAPE

After a while some of the Jews plotted together to kill him. They were watching for him day and night at the city gate so they could murder him, but Saul was told about their plot. So, during the night, some of the other believers lowered him in a large basket through an opening in the city wall.
ACTS 9:23-25

As the plane touched down in New Zealand, I thanked God again for his mercy in keeping me alive. My Christian friends, John and Reena, who had heard me speak at their church during one of my previous visits, generously provided for me with room and board. They adopted me as their spiritual son and told me their home was my home. Like a mother, Reena cared for me, washing my sandy clothes and showered motherly tenderness upon me. In addition to this loving couple, an entire group of believers dedicated to my safety and spiritual edification stood by my side. Fong and Dr. Maria hosted and organized this group. They fasted and prayed for and with me and generously provided for all my needs. Their love and generosity extended beyond the limits of the seas.

The Great Commission is to make disciples of every nation, and I was committed to doing all I could to reach Muslims for Christ. Rising early, I stepped forth once again onto New Zealand's beautiful soil to seek the lost and share the Good News. Along the way, I met a Muslim restaurant owner. Each day, I took time to demonstrate the love of Christ to him by not only giving him the Gospel, but also by helping him wash his many dishes, for Christ's love is best displayed in loving servitude. I met many other Muslims in my travels—some receptive, others not—and continued to spread the Gospel to countless more via a video app.

HUNTED AGAIN?

New Zealand had begun to feel like the safest place on earth when I suddenly received word that the religious police were looking for me in both Saudi and Dubai: two governments carrying out a full-scale investigation into my whereabouts with a bounty placed on my head as well as an international request to hand me over for execution by beheading. My brothers and sisters and I immediately began praying, asking God to blind the eyes of my enemies. And God answered.

Gulf State police incorrectly figured and presumed they were looking for an American according to news reports while the Saudi government issued a press release, lying about the things that had happened to me, insisting all reports were part of a giant hoax. This is the exact same thing they did following the death of Saudi journalist Jamal Khashoggi. God had temporarily confused the enemy, but it was not over yet.

Before I knew it, two New Zealand undercover police officers (likely paid by the Saudis) were snooping around the home of my hosts. So I fled and began jumping between the homes of various believers. New Zealand is a country known for its protection of religious freedom, but such freedoms can be quickly compromised wherever the love of money is greater than the love of liberty. I have firsthand knowledge of other Saudi Christians being kidnapped by the Saudi government while seeking refuge in New Zealand and some members of the New Zealand government turning a blind eye. This was no secret. New Zealand's media had reported widely on such travesties.

"If they want to take you," declared my New Zealand mother in Christ, "they'll first have to go through my dead body!"

Praise God for such nurturing, comforting motherly love!

To end this chase, I approached the officers and agreed to meet with them so long as we spoke at my Christian parents' house with both of them present as witnesses.

Sitting across from the officers, one of them looked me dead in the eye and asked me, "Are you a Christian?"

I nearly fell out of my chair! Is Christianity a crime? Was New Zealand no longer a defender of religious freedom?

"We will not tell the Saudi government," he continued, speaking in as friendly a tone as I sensed he could muster.

In my mind, I heard the voice of Jesus: "Behold, I am sending you out as sheep in the midst of wolves, so be wise as serpents and innocent as doves" (Mt 10:16, ESV).

It was then I noticed one of the interrogators attempt to sneakily record the conversation on a cell phone. The trap was being laid, so I offered only vague answers. Eventually my New Zealand mother interrupted the officer's line of questioning.

"He's a man of godly character! I testify to this. He has done nothing wrong, so why are you interrogating him?"

With no legal grounds to arrest me, the officers rose to leave. However, as they did so, one of them snuck an illegal photo of me.

I decided not to say anything.

A VISA?

Asylum in New Zealand was no longer an option. I had come to New Zealand because it was supposed to be a haven of religious freedom. Sadly, I came to understand that this freedom is quite limited. Pressure from the Saudi government had turned arms of welcome and safety into a deadly snare.

"Perhaps the Saudi government is ashamed that you are seeking asylum here," suggested the New Zealand man who had led me to Christ. "Don't apply," he advised. "They might kidnap you as they did the other believer who was with me. I fear that person is now dead."

With asylum off the table, this man encouraged me to apply for a different type of visa. Per the requirements, I needed to have been accepted at an English Language Institute. We went to one, but I didn't have enough money to pay up front. My friend and I were then directed to visit the owner of the institute. He was not Christian, but rather a Buddhist.

"Please, take a seat," said the director when we arrived at his office which was lined end-to-end in Buddhist symbols.

My friend spoke first.

"Ahmed, my friend here, doesn't have enough money to pay up front for the school. Can you please help us?"

Puzzled, the director said, "All of my Saudi Arabian students have plenty of money! Why are you so poor?"

"I am a hunted man," I explained. "Taking my money is but a fraction of what the Saudi government has done to me thus far."

"Why? What's your story?"

I told the director about the atrocities that had happened to me. I told him about the encounter in Auckland. I told him how I'd gone from being a respected doctor to a pauper simply because I follow Christ. To my surprise, even before I had finished speaking, tears were running like rivers down his cheeks.

"I will do whatever I can to help you," he said.

God had used my story to touch his heart. Here was a Buddhist who was willing to help me, a Christian, for free, just because of what Jesus had done for me.

TIME TO FLEE

Unfortunately, it soon became evident that, even with the director's aid, a visa was not a viable option for me either. This land of milk and honey was no longer a safe refuge.

"We know a Christian official in the government," said my precious New Zealand friend in a last-ditch effort to help.

We drove for hours to meet with him and share my story. A few days later, he contacted us.

"You must leave New Zealand at once," he said gravely. "Have you a travel visa to any other country?"

It was clear that he was trying to protect me so that I would not be sent back to Saudi Arabia and certain death. He informed me that the New Zealand government would soon order me to go to the Saudi embassy to fill out official documents for a visa. I couldn't believe my ears! They wanted me to go to my demise, to meet the Saudi government to be cut into pieces! This is no theory. Jamal Khashoggi—the U.S journalist originally from Saudi—was assassinated and dismembered in 2018 after being directed to a Saudi consulate for documentation. This alone is proof that the Saudi government lies to lure and then destroy its dissident citizens. I knew Jamal. He and I were in contact for almost a year before his murder during which time I shared with him the Good News of Jesus though he was not interested.

This order was a blatant threat, and I knew I would not return alive from such a visit, so I refused. The Saudi government then tried to buy me out. Knowing that I had no possessions, they offered me a full scholarship and monthly pay for me and any future spouse in exchange for my silence and cutting all ties with Christianity. My reply was brief, "Nothing can separate me from the love of God, not even your worthless money."

I had now but one prudent option: flee to the most powerful nation on earth, America. My hunters would not dare hunt me there.

With many tears and great sorrow, I said goodbye to my New Zealand family. My parting was especially difficult on my spiritual mother whose grief completely broke my heart.

"This is not goodbye," I said, trying to comfort her. "We'll be together soon!"

I went to purchase an airline ticket online, but every time I selected a seat, my choice was declined. After two hours on the phone with the airline's help center, I was told they would be unable to assist me and that I needed to consult in person with someone at the airport. I arrived the next day with the man who had led me to Christ in Auckland.

After a long wait, the woman at the counter called her supervisor who said, "Sorry, we have already allocated a seat for you."

I was dumbfounded!

The supervisor then handed me a ticket on which he circled a series of letters: SSSS.

He said nothing else.

A boarding pass marked with the letters SSSS (Secondary Security Screening Selection) means you are, quite literally, marked for a thorough examination. This code indicates your name is on a highly classified roster, the "Selectee List."

I looked at my spiritual father, my mind racing with thoughts of the horrors to come. We prayed, and then I quickly erased everything from my phone. I did not want to endanger anyone connected to me. My spiritual father continued in prayer as we walked to the immigration department.

The immigration officer smiled at every passenger, wishing them a safe flight. Then came my turn.

She smiled the same smile at me and asked, "Whereabouts are you heading today, sir?"

S.O.S.

"To the United States of America," I answered, matching her smile and handing her my passport.

Still smiling, she swiped my passport with her machine. All at once, her smile disappeared. Her pupils dilated. Something serious had appeared on her screen. With a robotic movement, she slowly picked up the phone and whispered something. Before I knew what was happening, a swarm of immigration officers had surrounded me. They seized my passport and ordered me to follow them. Using my smartwatch, I sent an S.O.S. message asking the believers to pray. I was sure my course had been diverted from America to the Kingdom of Saudi Arabia. But, trusting that God's plan was perfect whatever was to come, I calmly and confidently walked to the interrogation room.

No sooner had the door slammed behind me than was I hurled into a chair. Questions were spat from every direction, like a hail of missiles. Amid the intense bombardment, I managed to request a lawyer, but my request was denied as I was on international soil.

"Why do you think you're so special?" snarled one of the officers.

"Because I believe in Jesus," I answered.

"Since when do you believe in Jesus?" barked another.

Taking a breath, I began to tell them my testimony of my faith in Jesus Christ. I was prepared to be handed over to my enemies, ready to die; but first, I wanted this to be recorded. And so it was recorded: a joyful recounting of all the Lord had done for me.

After four hours of intense interrogation, it seemed I was being purposely delayed from boarding the flight to freedom.

"You are profiled as an extremist Christian," they said, "unwelcome in New Zealand. But," they continued, "we will allow you to travel to the U.S. You have not broken any laws, and that we will honor."

15 | FREEDOM

I will be glad and rejoice in your unfailing love, for you have seen my troubles, and you care about the anguish of my soul. You have not handed me over to my enemies but have set me in a safe place.
PSALM 31:7-8

Two officers escorted me to the boarding gate and then to my seat on the plane. Every eye along the way regarded me with varying degrees of interest and alarm. Once they'd stuffed me between two giant Samoan passengers who appeared to me to be flight marshals, the twelve-hour flight began. The marshals never moved once during the entire trip, not even to use the restroom, which in turn meant I didn't use the restroom either. Furthermore, there was an empty seat next to one of them which would have allowed both sets of gigantic shoulders, and my compressed chest, plenty of room to breathe. Alas, they elected the Ahmed sandwich seating arrangement. Though I never saw these men again, their crushing presences left an indelible (and probably physical) impression on my heart.

When we touched down in the United States, I began to prepare myself for the cavity search that was sure to occur; even still, my soul heaved a sigh of great relief to be at last on American soil. I approached the immigration officer expecting the worst—if New Zealand had detained me for four hours, how much longer would the United States hold me in interrogation?

"How are you doing today?" asked the officer, cheerfully.

"Fine," I replied, speaking as one bracing for a charging bull to make impact. "How are you?"

"Great!" she said with a smile. "Now, if you'll please place your fingers here, on this scanner, we'll need your prints."

I did so. And then, after quickly stamping my passport and handing it back to me, she said, "Welcome to America!"

I froze.

After a few moments with my eyes darting from left to right, wondering from which angle the surprise attack was coming, my brain declared, "Seriously? You are not going to interrogate me? You people must love extremist Christians like me!"

Noticing my still frozen state, the officer touched me warmly on the sleeve and said, "Sir, you are free to go."

"Thank you so much!" I cried so loudly it could almost have been called a squeal.

Finally, I thought, I'm free!

A CHANCE FOR ASYLUM IN THE U.S.A.

Step one had been getting to America; this accomplished, I now had to find shelter and provisions. I contacted some of the Christians who had come to know Christ during my last ministry visit to Fremont, California. They took me in gladly and cared for me for several months during which time I spoke in churches, encouraged my brothers and sisters in Christ, and continued my online evangelism.

I had been issued a six-month visa, so I hired a Christian lawyer and applied for asylum with Homeland Security on Good Friday, 2018. More than twenty people from around the world sent affidavits, testifying of my Christian faith and stating their knowledge or firm belief that a return to Saudi Arabia would mean execution for me under their apostasy laws. As a previous observer of such beheadings, neither I nor any of my sworn witnesses had any doubt this would happen to me. Additionally, through the Freedom of Information Act, I had evidence of the international request for my extradition to Saudi as well as the government of New Zealand's rejection of said request.

Less than a month later I was contacted by my lawyer.

"I have some very unusual news for you," he said. "You have a meeting with Homeland Security in just a few weeks. Normally," he continued, tension growing in his voice, "a person could wait four—maybe five—years for a meeting with USCIS. I've never seen anything like this. No one gets a meeting less than a month after applying! This could be really good, or really bad."

Slowly, I hung up the phone.

Good or bad? Whatever happens, it's all good (Rom 8:28)! On a human level, however, I would soon find out that it was very bad. My asylum case was denied.

As I thought about the process, I was not really surprised that I was not granted asylum. Many protocols were violated in my interview. Upon my arrival, the immigration officer called me by my full name, right there in public, announcing my name to all in the lobby of the U.S. Homeland Security office. My lawyer was shocked and immediately looked at me and said, "He's not supposed to do that! That's a violation of your privacy!"

"What can I do?" I said.

We stepped into the interview room, and my lawyer attempted to present a video of me in Mecca praying in the name of Jesus and evangelizing the Muslims there, but the immigration officer refused to look at it. My lawyer insisted this was important evidence demonstrating my faith in Jesus and cause for the Saudi government to sentence me to death. Still the officer was not in the least bit interested.

The interview began. With cold, terse speech, the officer shuffled through my traumatic memories, showing no sympathy, even indifference, as he did so. I offered a concise account of many of the happenings such as are recorded in this book: my upbringing in the center of Islam in Mecca, my conversion to Christianity at 19 years old, the great persecution I faced in the Gulf States, the countless beatings at the hands of the religious police, and the torture, proven by the scars I showed him, like the ones on my body or the ones on my face staring back at him. I talked about the many attempts on my life, beginning with the one committed by my own father and ending with my being hunted by Islamic terrorists, who, on two occasions, had pursued me with an SUV and machinegun fire while driving.

So much evidence had been presented ahead of time: twenty-one affidavits from eyewitnesses, videos of some of the incidents, printouts of my blocked websites, and piles of photos, all corroborating what I had now repeated in this interview. It was clear this officer had not prepared for my interview nor had he studied any of the evidence whatsoever.

In the middle of the interview, the officer began saying things like, "Your testimony is not believable. I do not believe you." Speaking at times with a cruel, mocking tone he challenged, "You are making this up so that you can stay in the U.S." He at last, laying a most improper accusation on the table said, "You are not a real Christian, are you?"

The interview continued for more than two hours in this most painful manner. Finally, once the officer had decided he'd had enough, he rose and grabbed my lawyer's hand, pulled him near, and began to whisper in his ear. My lawyer later told me that, in so many words, the officer had expressed his belief that I was a liar. He then turned to me and said, "Come back in two weeks. We'll have your decision then."

I left that day with a sinking feeling of foreboding. At the conclusion of two weeks, I got the news: Asylum Denied. With great incredulity, I read the following:

> Applicants for asylum must credibly establish that they have suffered past persecution or have a well-founded fear of future persecution on account of race, religion, nationality, membership in a particular social group, or political opinion and that they merit a grant of asylum in the exercise of discretion.
>
> For the reason(s) indicated below, USCIS has not granted your application for asylum:
>
> *Past Persecution*
>
> You have not established that any harm you experienced in the past, considering incidents both individually and cumulatively, amounts to persecution.
>
> *Future Persecution*
>
> You have not established that there is a reasonable possibility you would suffer persecution in the future.

Twenty-one affidavits from eyewitnesses affirming my Christian testimony, video and photos, and numerous past persecutions including tortures and attempted murders, evidenced even down to the mangled flesh of my back and scars on my face, were not deemed sufficient proof! Furthermore, Saudi law explicitly states that any Saudi national who does not follow Islam will be executed. A return to Saudi Arabia would mean certain death. Yet, the officer displayed an unjust and unprofessional bias, denying the mountain of proof set before him. Moments like this can make one feel helpless and defeated, too weak to forge ahead, but the Bible teaches us that in our weakness, Christ's strength is most evident (2 Cor 12:10).

Indeed, I was especially weak because even some Christians doubted my story. Some said, "His story is not true!" Others whispered behind my back, "The U.S. government knows more than us; that's why they rejected his case." Instead of showing me compassion and praying for me, they judged my heart like Job's unkind friends. Though I felt forsaken, I was not alone. I cried to the Lord, "Vindicate me Jesus, for I have told nothing but the truth." He heard my prayer.

Thankfully, the United States of America is still the land of the free and the home of the brave. It's the land that sheltered the Puritans when they'd fled persecution, a country governed by the rule of law—and, because of that rule, I had an opportunity to appeal my case and did so immediately.

AN ACT OF CONGRESS

I was referred to another attorney near Washington D.C., a specialist and expert in immigration cases like mine.

Upon reviewing the first decision, she declared, "This demonstrated a clear bias. Anyone can plainly see that Saudi Arabia has crushing persecution against any of its citizens who convert to Christianity."

She filed on my behalf with the U.S. Immigration office and recommended that I enlist my friends around the United States for help in contacting their elected representatives. How this would work, I had not a clue, but I put my complete trust in the Lord that he would do what was right according to his will. I was surrendered and submitted to Jesus, no matter what.

We laugh when we say some things take an act of Congress to get done. Well, my second interview really did take an act of Congress! My American brothers and sisters in Christ began contacting their congressional representatives and senators. After a relatively brief span of waiting, I opened my mailbox to find a letter addressed to me by a United States senator, pledging to work on my behalf. In fact, several U.S. senators and congressmen filed a congressional inquiry on my behalf. What was most amazing was the fact that they were from different political parties! Pulled from opposite sides of the aisle, they were now working together under the direction of my heavenly Father! To my joy, I received a swift response from the Office of U.S. Immigration:

> Mr. Joktan's file was requested back from the Office of Chief Counsel, and the file has been reviewed. Mr. Joktan has been scheduled for an additional asylum interview on [date] at the [US city] Asylum Office.

We appealed to Congress, and because of the prayers of God's people around the world, I was granted a second interview. That "act of Congress" was yet another miracle God has done for me. My attorney was astonished! Normally it takes several months to get a response from a congressional inquiry—but we serve a great and mighty God!

My lawyer arrived from Washington, D.C. Together with my pastor and a few friends, we were briefed on what to expect and how to prepare for the following day. I knew the Lord of all justice—the God of Daniel, Shadrach, Meshach, and Abednego—would have his way in the courts of man.

We arrived early at the immigration office, and, after going through security, we immediately noticed that they had reconfigured the waiting room in such a manner as to protect the privacy of asylum applicants, per my lawyer's request. To our delight, we also found that a new officer had been assigned to my case, one extremely more accommodating and incredibly kind. Whereas the previous officer was not at all familiar with my case, and quite antagonistic, this new officer said he had intently read all the now forty-some affidavits attesting to my faith in Jesus Christ and the severe persecution in the land of my childhood and beyond. He was very caring and careful to get the precise details of my situation.

I testified of my faith in Christ for over two hours. My pastor also testified, sharing firsthand information of my persecution and providing them with strong and compelling eyewitness evidence gathered from people who had seen my shot-up car, as well as those who'd trained me in evangelism in California.

After a total of three hours, my attorney made her closing statements. From all that we could tell, my interview could not have gone better. Before departing, our group joined hands in the waiting room to give glory and praise to God who had shown me his mercy and favor for the cause of the name of Jesus. We were rejoicing! Our prayer concluded with a joyful "Amen." When we lifted our eyes, we saw a worker from the immigration office listening to us.

"I just want to add my Amen to your prayer," she said. "It was beautiful. God touched me deeply. Thank you."

"Praise the Lord!" my pastor cried.

"Praise the Lord!" she cheered in return.

Wow! God's people are everywhere!

Not even a day later, my asylum case was accepted, and I am now under the legal protection of the United States of America! Usually this process can take up to several years, but in my case, it took less than one day. The Almighty heard our prayers and his protection and provision is beyond imagination! I say with David in Psalm 118:

> Let all who fear the Lord repeat: "His faithful love endures forever." In my distress I prayed to the Lord, and the Lord answered me and set me free. The Lord is for me, so I will have no fear. What can mere people do to me? Yes, the Lord is for me; he will help me. I will look in triumph at those who hate me. It is better to take refuge in the Lord than to trust in people. It is better to take refuge in the Lord than to trust in princes. Though hostile nations surrounded me, I destroyed them all with the authority of the Lord. Yes, they surrounded and attacked me, but I destroyed them all with the authority of the Lord. They swarmed around me like bees; they blazed against me like a crackling fire. But I destroyed them all with the authority of the Lord. My enemies did their best to kill me, but the Lord rescued me. The Lord is my strength and my song; he has given me victory.

A WIFE FROM ABOVE

There is one important detail that I will mention only in passing. It is the best part. While in the U.S., the Lord granted me one of the desires of my heart: a beautiful, godly woman who has stood faithfully by my side. Of course, behind every great romance is an amazing love story, especially when the Lord is involved. And I want to tell you that story!

The Bible tells us that "every perfect gift is from above, coming down from the Father of lights" (Jas 1:17, ESV), and this includes the gift of marriage.

Seeing that my youthful years were slipping away, my pastor encouraged me to get married. I told him that I had not yet found anyone suitable, to which he replied that God would make a way, that he had in store a precious gift just for me. But what female would marry a disfigured man, I wondered? Especially one who had formerly been a Muslim.

Answer: my wife.

I remember the first time I saw her. Our acquaintance began through an online dating site that my pastor helped set up. I humorously wrote that whoever was reading my page could blame my pastor. I added, for a date to occur, I would like for each of us to quote our favorite chapter from the Bible.

After several weeks of conversing digitally, I suggested we should meet face-to-face. We organized a group: she brought a friend who would later be one of our bridesmaids, and I brought my pastor, who is such a dear and close a friend to me that he's practically family.

The four of us went to dinner, and there, just as she said she would, my future wife recited a whole chapter of Scripture, Romans 8; for it was my desire that whomever I courted was serious about the Lord. Likewise, in a later get-together, I recited 2 Corinthians 4. This began a period in which we got to know each other thoroughly, through open discussions about the important things, from who Jesus is to each of us to what we believe a healthy marriage should look like. While we weren't planning to get married from day one, our relationship moved quickly in that direction. We each had an accountability partner (mine was my pastor, and hers was a mature Christian woman from her church) who helped us think Biblically about our relationship and honor God in our actions.

For her sake, my life needed to be entirely transparent; so, only a few weeks after our first online meeting, my pastor gave her the story of my life in the form of a first draft of this very book. I wondered if my past life as a Muslim would be a hindrance or distraction to our relationship. As it turns out, she received me as a true brother in Christ, dead to my old life and alive in the Lord.

The day finally came to meet her parents. She had told them long before our meeting about my history, that I am a Muslim from Saudi Arabia turned Christian; and to that, according to my wife, her father declared, "He says he's a Christian. But I'll tell you one thing: a Muslim would never eat pork. He has a test to pass. He must eat pork in front of me! Then I'll believe he's truly not a Muslim anymore!"

He didn't know, but since becoming a Christian, pulled pork has become one of my favorite foods.

We met for lunch, and her dad wasted no time in initiating his test. He ordered pork chops.

I said to the waitress, "I'll take exactly what he ordered."

Though I was excited for the meal, I was unaware that it came with a big container of incredibly salty sauce. Thinking nothing of it, I poured the entire container all over my pork chops. But, wanting to gain her father's approval, I joyfully ate every salty bite!

I then shared my testimony of faith. Her father was moved, but perhaps more impressed with my appetite for salty pork. As I concluded, he gave me his approval, saying "Okay! He's in!"

My father-in-law would later tell me that he'd liked me from the moment he saw me, and that I was an answer to his prayers for a godly man to marry his daughter.

We set a date for a wedding in late summer—this was before my first asylum interview, when we'd believed I had a "slam dunk" case. When the case was turned down, I gave her complete freedom to end our courtship and walk away; she would not. On three occasions, I asked her if she felt our relationship was truly the will of God. And three times, she said yes!

Our wedding day finally arrived. What a joy to have a wife who is a true friend, a sister in Christ, and a helper in the ministry! I am not worthy to be married to such a godly woman.

My forever family came from all around the world that day. Bryan, the pastor who first shared the gospel with me, agreed to officiate our wedding. Our pastors from our local churches helped with the rest of the ceremony. Although I'm disowned by my own Saudi family, my forever family in Jesus from all around the world took on the role of my true family and stood by my side on my wedding day. People had come to join the celebration from all over Africa, Asia, the Middle East, Europe, Australia, and New Zealand. It was like heaven on earth with people from every tribe, language, family, and nation. What a joy as well to have the honor of baptizing my wife the day after our wedding and to walk together in the light of Christ.[16]

ROMAN CITIZENSHIP

Paul had Roman citizenship that he used to the advantage of Christ's kingdom. Today's version is U.S. citizenship. After gaining asylum, I am on my way to being a part of the greatest nation on earth.

This world is not my home. As a Christian, my "citizenship is in heaven, from which we also eagerly wait for the Savior, the Lord Jesus Christ" (Phil 3:20). But while I'm on this earth, I am so grateful for the privileges and shelter I have been granted by this beloved nation, my adopted home country. There is a rule of law in America that is based on the Judeo-Christian ethic. Through the protections afforded me under the U.S. constitution, including freedom of religion, I am able to do what I was not able to do when I lived in Saudi: preach the Gospel freely and openly to every creature. This includes using new cyber technologies that allow me to be in Saudi and many other places through video and audio, evangelizing, discipling, and assisting in church planting, even though I cannot be there physically.

---

[16] Raised in the faith all her life as a Presbyterian, Ahmed's wife decided to be baptized by immersion.

16 | DUTIES TO THE LOST

*My ambition has always been to preach the Good News
where the name of Christ has never been heard.*
ROMANS 15:20

How does a Muslim come to the Lord Jesus Christ? It is certainly not flesh and blood that reveals Christ (Mt 16:17; 2 Cor 4:4). The same Spirit that helped me understand the Gospel is the same Spirit who must open the spiritual eyes of the Muslim world through the Word of God. "Of his own will he brought us forth by the word of truth" (Jas 1:18a, ESV).

When you meet an ordinary Muslim, most are not at all radical. However, if you were to inquire about their faith, they would most likely refer you to a leader in Islam, an imam (like a pastor), someone far more versed in the Quran. Almost all Islamic leaders lean toward extreme doctrine and attack the beliefs of Christianity, just as the Quran and the Islamic traditions (Hadith) instruct them to do.

Jesus commands us to be wise as serpents and harmless as doves (Mt 10:16). We are not to throw our precious pearls of truth to the pigs and dogs because they will turn on us and tear us apart (Mt 7:6). How then are we to properly evangelize the lost? Whether Muslim, atheist, or a professing Christian, we are called to love the lost. "Anyone who does not love does not know God, because God is love" (1 Jn 4:8).

We begin to experience God's passion for the lost when we remember and act in accordance with Jesus' persistent command to love: Love God with your whole heart (Mt 22:37); love your neighbor (Mt 22:39); love one another as God's family (Jn 13:34-35); even love your enemies (Mt 5:44).

1 Corinthians 13 is the most profound explanation of love: "Love is patient and kind. Love is not jealous or boastful or proud or rude. It does not demand its own way. It is not irritable, and it keeps no record of being wronged. It does not rejoice about injustice but rejoices whenever the truth wins out. Love never gives up, never loses faith, is always hopeful, and endures through every circumstance" (13:4-7).

As regards evangelism, we must remember that love is never rude to a person and act accordingly. We must always approach a lost soul bearing deep respect for that person, for they are made in God's image and loved dearly by him.

Jesus communicated with people according to his or her own level of understanding. He met people where they were. Among Jews, he spoke in a manner compelling to their intellectual minds, citing the laws they knew well and demonstrating the perfect fulfilment of those laws in him. With Gentiles, he spoke not as he did with Jews, about laws they'd never been taught nor followed, but rather in a manner practical to their lives, touching their understanding by relating himself and his work to the things they knew from their day-to-day lives, like farming or shepherding. Jesus always found common ground with the lost to reconcile them to the Father. He is our personal teacher (Mt 23:10) and example for reaching the lost.

I greatly admire Paul for his balance of gentleness and boldness. Consider Romans 1 in which he commends the admirable qualities and actions of the people, as likewise he did in Acts 17. By connecting with people on their level, showing them that he cared enough about them to get to know them intimately, he could effectively communicate the Good News. So, why are we trying to invent a new way to reach people for Christ? Aren't the examples of Jesus and the apostles enough? The Gospel has not changed. The Good News has lost none of its power. And the gates of hell will never prevail against Christ's Kingdom.

"But how can they call on him to save them unless they believe in him? And how can they believe in him if they have never heard about him? And how can they hear about him unless someone tells them? And how will anyone go and tell them without being sent? That is why the Scriptures say, 'How beautiful are the feet of messengers who bring good news!'" (Rom 10:14-15). Muslims are killing and being killed for the salvation of their souls. Who will share the Gospel with them? Who will introduce to them the true Isa? Whose responsibility is it to evangelize them? What is your responsibility and mine?

WHAT IS OUR DUTY TO THE LOST?

The god of this world is in control of those who do not believe in Jesus. He is blinding their eyes (2 Cor 4:4). Jesus said, "Your eye is like a lamp that provides light for your body.

When your eye is healthy, your whole body is filled with light. But when your eye is unhealthy, your whole body is filled with darkness. And if the light you think you have is actually darkness, how deep that darkness is!" (Mt 6:23). How amazing that Jesus can open blind eyes! He said, "I am the light of the world. If you follow me, you won't have to walk in darkness, because you will have the light that leads to life" (Jn 8:12).

Right now, Muslims all over the world think that killing a Christian means serving Allah. They cry out, "Allahu Akbar!" (Allah is greater) when they murder in his name. But our Lord Jesus, who predicted such happenings two thousand years ago, offered comfort amid this evil saying, "For you will be expelled from the synagogues [places of congregating], and the time is coming when those who kill you will think they are doing a holy service for God" (Jn 16:2). And why did Jesus say this thousands of years ago? "I have told you these things so that you won't abandon your faith" (Jn 16:1).

We must not run away from speaking the truth to those who persecute us, for we are, very likely, the only ones who will tell them of Jesus' love. We must go as Jesus commands us, "Go therefore and make disciples of all nations, baptizing them in the name of the Father and of the Son and of the Holy Spirit, teaching them to observe all that I have commanded you. And behold, I am with you always, to the end of the age" (Mt 28:19-20, ESV).

This command does not mean "go to church" or "go to Bible study," even though these are good things. Rather, Jesus commands us to leave our comfort zones and boldly proclaim his name to those who have never heard of it or his plan of salvation. We must be willing to risk our lives, our wealth, our reputation—everything!—for the sake of the cross and the lost Jesus has called to come to it.

There are many Christians who do indeed leave safe countries, like the U.S., to work in dangerous places, like Saudi Arabia. They set out with great zeal, wanting to tell others about the Good News of Jesus having died to give us life. But, sadly, too many get caught up in work responsibilities and the pressures of making money, neglecting this high calling. Fear easily takes hold. They know that if they are caught speaking of Jesus, they will lose their jobs and immediately be sent back to their home country. Some may even lose their lives, but this should not discourage Christians from evangelizing.

Christians who go to places like my home country must preach the Gospel regardless of the consequences because our God is Jehovah-Jireh, the God who provides for all our needs. If we obediently go to work for him, we may suffer loss, but he will provide. We need to have the attitude of our Savior in Matthew 9:36-38 (ESV): "When he saw the crowds, he had compassion for them, because they were harassed and helpless, like sheep without a shepherd. Then he said to his disciples, 'The harvest is plentiful, but the laborers are few; therefore pray earnestly to the Lord of the harvest to send out laborers into his harvest.'" Often those who pray for laborers become the laborers whom God sends.

Most likely, none of the 9/11 terrorists had ever heard that Jesus had died for their sins. What if the Christians working all around the Islamic world had shared the love of Christ with them? The Lord can save anyone, but "how will they hear without a preacher?" (Rom 10:14). We must not focus on the world's treasures—money, power, prestige, or the latest hot item—but instead focus on laying up treasures in heaven where moth and rust have no power to destroy.

What then should be our response? You don't have to go to a Muslim country to obey the Great Commission. Go to the mosques in your hometown or neighborhood and tell them the Gospel in a spirit of love and truth, obeying the second greatest commandment: to love our neighbors as ourselves. How selfish we are to hide the riches of Christ and not offer eternal life to all our neighbors, including Muslims! Jesus says we are the light of the world! We must let his light shine through us! A light must not be hidden under a basket!

Now that you have come to understand the great darkness and blindness enshrouding the over two billion Muslims of the world, I pray that today you will hear the Lord say, "Go!" In Mark 16:15, Jesus says, "Go into all the world and preach the Good News to everyone." If we disobey this call, a vast group of people will remain in darkness. Christ is a mighty Savior, able to save the most hardened sinners, and we are his hands and feet. It is his will for us to proclaim his Gospel to the world, including two billion Muslims, to bring them to Christ.

When the Son of Man returns, how many faithful will he find on the earth who have trusted in his words (Lk 18:8)? How many are obeying his command to "go"? Will he find you faithful?

WHAT CAN I DO RIGHT NOW?

Let us surrender anew to the power of Christ's love, forsaking our worldly dreams and ambitions. The Christian life is Christ. His heart beats in the chest of every believer. Let us stir ourselves up to proclaim the Gospel to everyone on earth, including Muslims. Following 9/11 and the advent of ISIS, Muslims are at last seeing the ugliness of their false religion and are coming to Christ in droves. Look at what the Lord is doing in the most difficult Muslim areas in the world! As Christian persecution spreads in Iran, Syria, Egypt, Nigeria, Uganda, and Mali, reports of millions of Muslims coming to Christ are widespread.

God is not willing that any should perish. Are you so willing? What can you do? Much:
- Pray for Muslims in Islamic countries around the world to come to Christ.
- Go on a short-term trip to Saudi Arabia and share Christ.
- Support missionaries and agencies (like Mecca to Christ International and the Navigators) that support evangelism to Muslims and send workers to Muslim countries.

A PARADIGM OF GRACE

How shall we reach the lost? There are many secondary beliefs and systematic theologies that divide Christians among denominational lines. Issues like baptism, church government, sign gifts, etc. are important things to understand and discuss among believers. But all Christians are united as one in Christ through the Gospel (Eph 2:11-22). We preach the same Gospel in all true Christian churches: Jesus is God and died to forgive sinners—paying the price we could never pay for all the wrong we've done. By so believing and asking the risen Christ to personally forgive every sin and to take over one's life, by faith in the fulfillment of this, anyone can be saved. Sinners can be made right before a holy God through the blood of Jesus. This is the Gospel.

Divisions

Some are willing to divide the Body of Christ for their own theological views. Their demands do not align with those of the Bible, and they promote an evangelism that is according to their way only. We can easily become tribal by promoting our preferred denominational theology ahead of Christ. This should not be so, for there is one Body only, composed of many parts.

Unity does not mean uniformity. Jesus prayed for unity in his prayer in John 17. We are to teach the Word, line upon line, precept upon precept. But we must not lose sight of the heart of the matter. We are not called to promote our own pet theologies and attack other Christians. If we are truly children of God, we should be living with a good conscience and be fully persuaded in our own minds about everything in the Word of God (Rom 14:5). And on secondary issues, we must first love one another. Humility is the essence of the Spirit's fruit. Anyone who does the will of our Father in heaven is our brother, sister, and mother (Mt 12:50). We must align ourselves in this manner with those who are truly born again in Christ, not by mere denominational beliefs.

Compromise

A red line has been drawn for us by the apostles: "Woe to me if I do not preach the Gospel" (1 Cor 9:16, ESV). The apostle Paul goes on to delineate that line: "I have become all things to all people, that by all means I might save some" (1 Cor 9:22).

Paul was committed to putting on the cultures of other peoples and nations, but he would never compromise the Gospel to do so. "Woe to me," he said, "if I compromise and do not preach the Gospel!"

Let us apply this principle to evangelizing Muslims. Allah simply means "god" in Arabic, but this does not mean that the Allah of the Quran and the God of the Christian Bible are the same being. If I want to reach Muslims through deceit, saying that Allah and Christ are one and the same as a compromise, I am equating a false god with the one true and living God. This would be akin to the compromise of Jeroboam who set up an altar to the golden calf and called that golden calf Yahweh (1 Kings 12:25-33).

Allah is no more God than was the golden calf; both are false gods and idols. However, quoting the Quran is not a compromise. My own conversion came through the bridge of using the Quran first! In fact, speaking to Muslims with knowledge of their sacred texts can make you more credible to them, keeping the conversational reins in your hands, and helping them understand who Isa is through the some of the verses imported into the Quran from the New Testament.

Grace

With that in mind we should have a paradigm of grace to all our fellow, truly born again, Gospel-preaching brothers and sisters in Christ spread far and wide around the world making up the church of Jesus. It is the central tenant of the Gospel that Jesus died for guilty sinners, to justify and forgive them before a holy God. Anyone who looks to Jesus as Savior, trusts in his death on the cross, and believes he was raised from the dead for our salvation will be saved. What is this grace? It's found in Mark 9:38-41:

> John said to Jesus, "Teacher, we saw someone using your name to cast out demons, but we told him to stop because he wasn't in our group." "Don't stop him!" Jesus said. "No one

who performs a miracle in my name will soon be able to speak evil of me. Anyone who is not against us is for us. If anyone gives you even a cup of water because you belong to the Messiah, I tell you the truth, that person will surely be rewarded.

Jesus speaks to all of us saying, I did not call you to fight with each other, but rather to go and share the Gospel. Debating theology or details is not the goal. Sound theology is absolutely necessary, but it is a means to an end. A person must be sound in the Gospel, but humility will teach us that we are all unsound in one area or another, even if we don't realize it. Let us have grace toward those who differ on secondary issues as long as they are clearly born again, committed to the clear Gospel, and know the love and grace of Jesus. If someone is advancing Christ's kingdom and not their own, we are not to stop anyone from proclaiming his name. God uses denominational churches as well as independent churches, but all true Christians are part of the Body of Christ. The unity of the Spirit must be the blood that runs through each of us.

17 | WHAT SHALL WE DO THEN?

Peter's words pierced their hearts, and they said to him and to the other apostles, "Brothers, what should we do?" Peter replied, "Each of you must repent of your sins and turn to God, and be baptized in the name of Jesus Christ for the forgiveness of your sins. Then you will receive the gift of the Holy Spirit. This promise is to you, to your children, and to those far away—all who have been called by the Lord our God." Then Peter continued preaching for a long time, strongly urging all his listeners, "Save yourselves from this crooked generation!" Those who believed what Peter said were baptized and added to the church that day—about 3,000 in all.
Acts 2:37-41

BY AHMED'S PASTOR

God is on the move and is saving people like Ahmed in Muslim countries every day. We know the power of God can be unleashed only through a clear and wise presentation of the Gospel. "How shall they hear without a preacher?" (Rom 10:14). This has been Ahmed's motivation in establishing a new ministry that is dedicated to reaching Muslims and people of all kinds with the Gospel of Jesus. Mecca to Christ International was founded during the asylum appeals of Ahmed Joktan in order to reach Muslims and all peoples with the love of Jesus, both in the U.S. and around the world. The message of the Gospel alone is powerful to save anyone who will believe.

STATISTICS

There are estimated to be upwards of 3 and a half million Muslims living in the United States, and that number is growing every year by 20,000.[17] Who will go? 100,000 in Dearborn, Michigan. 270,000 in state of New Jersey. 500,000 in Chicago. There are Muslim populations in all 50 states.

Around the world, the statistics are even more astounding. Today, there are more than 2 billion Muslims in the world, which is around 25% of the world's population. Worldwide, ten million Muslims convert to Christianity every year.[18] Who will reach them for the Lord Jesus Christ?

MECCA TO CHRIST INTERNATIONAL

Mecca to Christ International is dedicated to reaching Muslims for Christ in a variety of ways.

---

[17] Muhammad, Besheer. "A New Estimate of U.S. Muslim Population." Pew Research Center. January 03, 2018. Accessed September 27, 2018. http://www.pewresearch.org/fact-tank/2018/01/03/new-estimates-show-u-s-muslim-population-continues-to-grow/.

[18] Duane A. Miller. "Believers in Christ from a Muslim Background: A Global Census." Academia.edu. 2015. Accessed September 27, 2018. https://www.academia.edu/16338087/Believers_in_Christ_from_a_Muslim_Background_A_Global_Census.

US Evangelism

Ahmed and his team are committed to traveling to Muslim populations in the U.S. to spread the love of Jesus through evangelism of all sorts: visiting people door-to-door, visiting college campuses, and going everywhere proclaiming the Gospel. Obviously, we are called to evangelize every person so though Ahmed and his team have expertise with giving the good news to Muslims, they have a burden for all people in need of Christ.

Equipping Churches

Ahmed has a deep desire to see churches equipped to evangelize Muslims. He enjoys sharing firsthand in churches across the U.S. and the world of what the Lord has done in bringing him from Islam to Christ. This is also a time when churches can be trained in evangelism for various people groups, with a special emphasis on Muslim evangelism. We provide training and instruction on how to reach groups of all sorts. How do we reach Hindus, Jehovah's Witnesses, Atheists, etc., for Christ? It is our desire to equip the church to be bold and effective when approaching such groups and others in this pluralistic, post-modern world and give believers the tools to shine the light of Christ into every form of darkness.

Evangelism to Saudi Arabia

Although we have thankfully been able to send evangelism teams there since 2015, Saudi Arabia was a closed country for tourists until 2019. The prayer warriors living in Saudi prayed day and night for the strongholds of darkness to be lifted. They prayed for the Holy Spirit to advance the Gospel in Saudi. Nowadays we believe a window of opportunity has opened where the kingdom of Saudi Arabia is ready to receive the Gospel of Jesus Christ. We can now send tourists to Saudi with the Gospel.

Why send groups of Christians as missionaries to Mecca? First, Mecca is the birthplace of Islam. Every day, hundreds of thousands of Muslims journey to Mecca to do *Umrah* (visitation). Some of them come and go in the same day from their distant homes around the world. When Muslims come to Mecca, they come brokenhearted. These are not radical terrorists. They are normal, everyday people like you and me, sadly misguided by the false religion of Islam, who have sold everything to find God in Mecca that they might know the one who created them. They have been taught that God's house is in Mecca. They are not arrogant but rather ignorant of the true and living God. They are open to listening to almost anyone, making Mecca one of the greatest mission fields in all the world.

We want to reach Muslims in Mecca for Jesus Christ so that they too can spread the true Gospel around the world. Once they accept Christ, they can carry the seeds of truth to their own families and neighbors and become Christ's ambassadors. This is God's work: saving travelers to Mecca so that they can take the good news to their own people. Often, these Muslim nations are completely closed to Christian missionaries, but God can easily do the impossible. In this way, we can and will reach the farthest regions of the world for Christ.

In the first two years of Mecca to Christ International, we assisted over 800 short-term missionaries to Mecca, Saudi Arabia, from various regions around the world: the U.S., Europe, and Asia. How was this possible? What is impossible for man is possible for God. Christians who are not citizens of the Kingdom of Saudi Arabia are welcome to visit the Gulf States on short-term trips. This allows people from many nations to travel there with the Gospel in tow, and through the help of Christians working underground, short-term missionaries can preach the Good News.

Many people in this region already speak English, and those who don't can hear through an interpreter. Still, how is this possible? Isn't Christianity against the law? Yes and no. It is true that if a citizen of the Gulf States converts to Christianity, he or she can be put to death. However, foreigners are allowed to practice their faith privately. There is also an opening in the culture through which the Gospel can be preached to Muslims: the cultural mandate of hospitality. If you are a Christian visitor to Saudi Arabia and you meet a Muslim there, it is culturally proper for them to ask you three questions: 1) What is your name? 2) Where are you from? 3) What is your religion? This cultural value of welcoming you to their community is very important for Muslims. It is entirely proper after you introduce yourself, explain where you are from, let them know you are a Christian and proclaim the clear Gospel of Jesus.

Surprisingly, this method of Christian evangelism is perfectly aligned with Sharia law. Cultural hospitality dictates their asking a foreigner several important questions, and that foreigner by Saudi law has all the right to answer in any way he or she pleases. This is legal and is not considered proselytizing.

If you are interested in being a short-term or long-term missionary to Saudi Arabia, you are invited to request an application through Mecca to Christ International. We hope you will join our movement of obeying the Great Commission in this way. God sent his Son from heaven to earth to die for you and me so we could obtain unmerited grace. Please seriously consider how you can spread the Gospel to Muslims by proclaiming Christ in Saudi Arabia. You are God's plan A—he has no plan B!

Social Media Ministry

When Ahmed is not traveling, he is actively evangelizing through online ministries. He regularly proclaims Christ to Muslims through Muslim-geared social media apps. We also have an evangelistic website for those seeking Christ in Saudi Arabia and are currently seeking ministry partners who will help us send Arabic New Testaments to specific addresses throughout the Gulf States.

Publishing Ministry

Ahmed has a heart to produce materials that will both equip the church and evangelize Muslims. *From Mecca to Christ* is the inaugural book of Mecca to Christ International, but many more publications are planned.

Medical Outreach Ministry

We are trusting God for a medical team alongside Dr. Ahmed to one day go where Muslims have been devastated by war. We know that their only hope will come if we share the Gospel with them.

YOUR PART

Perhaps you cannot travel a great distance to proclaim Christ in Mecca. What can you do?

Pray. The greatest commitment you can make to advancing the Gospel of Jesus in Muslim communities is to pray specifically for those communities. Pray for the millions that travel on pilgrimage to Mecca every year that they would let go of their quest for Mecca and begin their journey with Christ. Pray for Muslims in your own community and ask God for ways that you can engage with them.

Be hospitable. Hospitality is a very important teaching in the Bible and a major part of Eastern culture, which has, in large part, been lost in the West. You can show hospitality to Muslims simply by being friendly to them. Look them in the eye with a smile and greet them with joy. Get to know them as friends. Invite them into your home. Show them the love of Christ before you teach them of His love. In the U.S., many look upon Muslims with suspicion due to the events of 9/11. Christians must show them the way of love—not just through words, but through deeds as well. There are also other ministries like Mecca to Christ through which you can help Muslim background believers with housing and other needs.

Get equipped. There are a few other ministries dedicated to training Christians to reach Muslims with the love of Jesus, like those of Nabeel Qureshi and Ravi Zacharias. Both have written several books worth reading that will help get you started in evangelizing Muslims. Beyond that, the ministry of Mecca to Christ would love to send Ahmed and his team to your church to not only train and equip the believers there, but to also take them out into your community and set up an evangelistic outreach.

Give! If you would like to give to Mecca to Christ International, you can partner with us through a one-time gift or regular financial support. Your partnership will help us connect Bible teachers with the persecuted church in Saudi and persecuted Christians in the Muslim world.

Go! Join a short or long-term missions trip. If you are able, please consider traveling to Mecca for the Kingdom of Jesus. It is one thing to pray for countries and nations to be saved, but it is another thing to obey Christ's command to go and preach the Gospel in faraway lands. If the Lord has given you the desire and ability to go to Mecca to pray, visit, and speak to needy Muslims, let us know. Some who visit can give a clear Gospel presentation, and others are able only to pray. Both are desperately needed to impact Muslims worldwide.

A FINAL WORD FROM AHMED

I am a living, breathing Christian, converted and rescued from Islam only because my Lord Jesus Christ died for me and rose again. He forgave me and transformed me by the power of his resurrection. He appeared to me, and I surrendered to him as Lord and trusted him as my only Savior. It is my desire that all people around the world would worship my Lord and Savior Jesus Christ. Will you join me in this quest to advance the Good News of Jesus worldwide?

Appendix 1 | ISLAM'S BEGINNINGS & TEACHINGS

He [Jesus] calls his own sheep by name and leads them out. After he has gathered his own flock, he walks ahead of them, and they follow him because they know his voice. They won't follow a stranger; they will run from him because they don't know his voice.

JOHN 10:3-5

On September 11, 2001, nineteen militants associated with the Islamic extremist group, al-Qaeda, hijacked four airplanes and carried out targeted suicide attacks in the deadliest terrorist attack on United States soil. Two planes were flown into the Twin Towers of the World Trade Center in New York City, a third plane hit the Pentagon just outside Washington DC, and a fourth plane crashed in a field in Pennsylvania. Just under 3,000 people were killed during the 9/11 attacks, including more than 400 police officers and firefighters. This act of terror, catalyzing nearly two decades of ongoing war, had been carried out in the name of Islam.

Why would several members of my own tribe desire to murder so many innocent people? How could anyone commit such heinous crimes in the name of Allah? To answer that question, let's take a look at the history of Islam.

THE ORPHAN SPIRIT OF ISLAM

Muhammad was born around 570 A.D. in the town of Mecca on the Arabian Peninsula, where Saudi Arabia is presently located. His father died before he was born, and, following his birth, Muhammad was given to a nurse who raised him away from his family for the first three to four years of his life. At age six, he suffered the great tragedy of losing his mother (Quran 93:6). His grandfather then took him in but died two years later, leaving Muhammad orphaned. He would thereafter be taken in by his uncle as a disgraced servant rather than an adopted child.

This difficult beginning would affect Muhammad's teaching to its core, for the spirit and attitude of Islam is one of orphanhood,[19] with a great lack of empathy at the root of the Quran's teachings. Muhammad's heart was broken, and his desperation and fatalism are reflected in his words. At the center of Islam is Muhammad's orphaned heart projected onto his understanding of Allah. Another important item to note concerning Muhammad's upbringing is this: throughout his childhood, it is believed he never received any formal education and was illiterate. All of his learning was done by oral memorization.

---

[19] Adoption in Islam was eventually made illegal because Muhammad wanted to marry his daughter-in-law from his adopted son Zaid (*cf* Quran 33:37-38). He also suffered as an orphan and, therefore, wanted others to taste the same suffering.

A RELIGION OF PEACE OR HATRED?

The desert environment and mountainous terrain around Muhammad were harsh, and the region was relatively isolated from the rest of the world. However, many religions were present in that region, with the cities of Mecca and Medina being filled with Jews and pagans. Only a few committed Christians lived in the Arabian Peninsula, but Christian monasteries and communities flourished along the surrounding trading routes. Frequent tribal warfare was prevalent, as well as the belief in supernatural beings such as angels, demons, and mystical creatures called *jinn*, or genies.

At about nine years of age, Muhammad went to what is now Syria for trading purposes. There, a Nestorian[20] Christian named Bahira (also known as Sergius the Monk) invited him for a meal at the local monastery where Muhammad was shown great kindness and hospitality. Early in the Quran, you can see the doublemindedness of its teaching, with both gratitude and love for Christians alongside hatred for Jews and pagans (*cf* Quran 5:82). This passage seems to recall the kind of treatment Muhammad received from the monk who'd helped him as a child; yet, in the same chapter, Muslims are told not to make friends with Christians or Jews (Quran 5:51). Muhammad seems torn between his fond memories of the Christian monk's benevolence toward him and his own desire to slaughter anyone not devoted to Allah: an internal struggle made clear throughout the Quran.

This explains why most Muslims around the world (roughly 70%) genuinely want to live in peace. Yet, radicalized

---

[20] Nestorianism taught that the human and divine natures of Jesus were so separated that Jesus of Nazareth was different from what he became when inhabited by the Spirit of Christ. The human and the divine were two different persons.

Muslims, perhaps 30% of Islam's followers, can read the same Quran and be filled with enough hatred to commit the crimes of 9/11. The Quran's teaching, as we will see, is not monolithic; it's quite contradictory and an accurate representation of Muhammad's confused and conflicted thinking.

MUHAMMAD'S WIVES & CHILDREN

As a young boy, Muhammad worked many different jobs. Since he came from a very poor family, and his uncle couldn't afford Muhammad's expenses, the young boy became a caretaker of livestock to earn money. For additional income, he maintained his tribe's idols and participated in many conflicts with neighboring tribes, enriching himself with the spoils of war. But all of that was not enough to feed young Muhammad's appetites for riches and social status. One day, he was presented with a tempting opportunity: the end of his poverty through a marriage into money.

When charming young Muhammad was twenty-five, Khadija—a wealthy widow fifteen years his senior—became captivated by his charisma and strength, eventually falling in love. She desired to marry him, but Muhammad didn't have enough money to pay her *muhar*[21] which would've caused embarrassment to his tribe. To his relief, she covered the cost with her extravagant wealth and the wedding was set.

Muhammad had previously worked as his wife's employee, traveling throughout the Arabian region and taking care of her business ventures. This first marriage was monogamous for twenty-five years, and the couple had six daughters

---

[21] Arabian tradition requires payment of money to the wife's family in order to get married, as a means of showing the man's financial capabilities.

together. Later, many of these daughters were married to Muhammad's successors who would divide Islam into two major sects: Sunni and Shiite. As we will see later in this book, this division was all about money, power, and control through Muhammad's family.

Following Khadija's death, Muhammad did not remain single very long. Now a man over fifty, Muhammad married six-year-old Aisha, the daughter of Muhammad's first religious successor, Abubaker. But one wife was not enough for this so-called prophet as he went on to marry more than ten other women, having up to nine wives at one time with plans to marry many more. In fact, the only barrier that limited this ambition was his own death. With so many lurid details swirling about these marriages, one could fuel a modern-day soap opera with enough twists, turns, and disturbing plot lines to stay on the air for decades.

Such disregard for the dignity of women, central to the very heart of the family structure presented in the Quran, further explains the hardening of conscience that takes place among Islam's followers. Given that the women married to Muhammad were treated as sex slaves and non-persons, it is no wonder the sociopathic seed of coldness and indifference would go on to breed a following of stone-cold killers.

THE INFLUENCE OF WARAKA IBN NAWFAL

In many ways, the core teachings of Islam come from a Messianic Jew by the name of Waraka ibn Nawfal, an uncle to the prophet Muhammad by his first wife, Khadija, who became one of his closest—and by far most influential— confidants. Waraka studied the Bible under Jews and Ebionite Christians and translated the New Testament into Arabic. Some Islamic sources imply that he may have also translated the Old Testament into Arabic. Ebionite Christians were from the region of Nazareth; but, much like the later Arians and modern-day Jehovah's Witnesses, they did not believe in the deity of Christ and were expelled to Arabia on the charge of heresy. Waraka was both a scholar and the primary leader of the Ebionites in Mecca. Unfortunately, nearly every bad religion comes out of a Christian cult.

The story of how Waraka and the boy Muhammad met is recounted by many of the secondary Muslim holy books (a collection of six primary books called the *Hadith*). In 576 A.D., Waraka found the lost five-year-old boy wandering around Upper Mecca. He took a special interest in the young Muhammad, seeing in him qualities of leadership. Waraka would spend a great deal of time with Muhammad over the years, teaching him the way of the Ebionites as well as the Torah; he even performed Muhammad's marriage to Khadijah and groomed him to take his place as the Ebionite Christian spiritual leader in Mecca.

When Muhammad, now about forty years old, first announced that he was receiving revelations from God, the revelations were in large part direct copies of the stories he had heard from Waraka ibn Nawfal, as one can observe from his pattern of speaking in the Quran.[22] Waraka encouraged Muhammad to consider himself a prophet, with the understanding that just as Moses had been the key prophet to call the

---

[22] Satan's devices are the same throughout the ages. For example, the book of Mormon is written in much the same pattern as the Quran with someone trying to recite and plagiarize another's teaching. Just as Joseph Smith robbed and regurgitated the Bible, slightly twisting names and places for the book of Mormon, the style of the Quran is clearly another person's work, as evidenced by the dramatic change in style of the portions of the Quran written after Waraka's death.

Jews back to God, and Jesus had been the prophet who'd called his generation back to God, so too would Muhammad be the prophet who would call the Arabs back to God. It is interesting to note that, at this time, Muhammad did not see himself as the founder of a new religion, rather as someone merely calling people back to the faith of Abraham, Moses, and Jesus.

THE DEMONIC INFLUENCE OVER MUHAMMAD

Often during times of revelation, Muhammad would be convulsing with deep tremors. This may point to evidence of demonic influence, possibly possession. Even as a boy, he would enter frequently into trances that one of his nurses attributed to demonic control. Later in his life, Muhammad admitted that he was possessed (Quran 17:47). The Quran speaks about black magic as heavenly teachings (Quran 2:102), bestowed by angels to help Muslims overcome their daily life struggles. It is believed these evil angels are the fallen angels spoken of in the Bible (Isa 14:12-15, Lk 10:18, Rev 12:7-17, 2 Pet 2:4).

Other evidence supporting the belief of demonic influence is found in the Quran itself. Twenty-nine chapters of the Quran begin with a mix of random, incoherent letters. Witchcraft in the Arabian Peninsula used words written backwards and letters were jumbled as a means of casting spells. It is possible that the random letters at the beginning of these chapters could be taken from spells familiar to Muhammad. The inhabitants of Arabia at that time also believed that *jinn,* or magical genies, inhabited dirty, deserted places such as abandoned homes and caves. When Muhammad received the first of his revelations, he was in a cave called Hira, and he believed he was afflicted by a demonic creature.[23]

Alone at night in the pitch darkness of an abandoned cave, something took hold of him, squeezed him tightly, and shook him three times. He was frightened by this supernatural experience and thought he was in the control of a fallen angel. Deeply alarmed, Muhammad made his way home where he was consoled by his wife Khadijah who persuaded him that the whole ordeal had actually been Allah calling him to be a prophet.

The demonic incidents continued as recorded in the Quran where Muhammad, while receiving revelations, spoke what he later claimed to be "Satanic verses." These verses were later annulled by Muhammad on the basis of being corrupted and influenced by Satan (*cf* Quran 22:52; 53:19-26).

THE DEATH OF WARAKA IBN NAWFAL

The influence of Waraka ibn Nawfal upon Muhammad and his revelations continued until Waraka's death. It is not accidental that the Hadith[24] writers note that "revelations ceased for some time" following the death of Waraka. The apparent reason is that Muhammad was no longer learning from his Ebionite uncle.

The death of Waraka ibn Nawfal, beneath whom Muhammad had dutifully studied for over fifteen years, was so dis-

---

[23] Again, we see Satan's schemes do not change. For example, Joseph Smith had a similar encounter with a spiritual being called Moroni, no doubt a demon similar to the one who appeared to Muhammad, sent by the father of all lies.

[24] *Hadith* refers to "What Muhammad said." They are secondary holy books that support the teachings of the Quran and contain the sayings, acts, or tacit approvals validly or invalidly ascribed to the Islamic prophet Muhammad.

tressing that Muhammad wanted to commit suicide as recorded in the most important collection of holy books of the Sunni Muslims after the Quran: the Hadith.[25] We read this in Sahih Hadith of Bukhari which was supposedly narrated by Aisha, his youngest wife:

> But after a few days, Waraka died, and the Divine Inspiration was also paused for a while, and the Prophet became so sad as we have heard that he intended several times to throw himself from the tops of high mountains in Mecca (Sahih al-Bukhari, Book 87, Hadith 111).

Because of Waraka's significance to Muhammad, the writings of the Quran fall into two stylistic genres: peaceful writing from Mecca and hateful, violent writing from Medina reflecting in their distinct styles the happenings of Muhammad's life.

The Quranic verses written in Mecca were influenced—and perhaps even dictated to Muhammad—by Waraka, who was always peaceful toward Christians and Jews. The Quranic verses written in Medina, however, were compiled after Waraka's death; and the style displayed in its verses, as well as its composition and grammar, show very clearly to have been penned entirely by a different author. Here, Muhammad was no longer reciting the teachings of his peaceful mentor; he was instead bleeding out his own hateful thoughts. As displayed in Medina, Muslims at that time were now the majority, and Muhammad is no longer interested in peace, but rather in war and *jihad* (holy war).

This understanding of Waraka's influence is vital to learning how Islam can be called a religion of peace, and yet have

---

[25] There are six canonical books in the Hadith and forty-two sub-canonical books.

some of its chief ideals be war, death, and hatred. The message of peace and living in harmony was twisted after Waraka's death into an attitude of hatred and desire for the destruction of all groups outside of Islam.

FROM PEACE TO WAR AFTER WARAKA'S DEATH

Encouraged by his wife Khadijah, Muhammad began to share his revelations with the inhabitants of Mecca after the death of Waraka in 610 A.D. Muhammad told them Allah alone was God and Muhammad was his messenger. He was met with nothing but disbelief because he had a constantly changing message at the time, and he was unable to perform the miracles they'd requested. Quran 16:101-102 speaks of this incident:

> When we substitute one revelation in place of another revelation – and Allah is most knowing of what He sends down – they say, 'You, O Muhammad, are but an inventor of lies.' But most of them do not know. Say, O Muhammad, 'The Holy Spirit has brought it down from your Lord in truth to make firm those who believe and as guidance and good tidings to the Muslims.'

In this instance, Muhammad blamed the Holy Spirit for the differing messages by saying, "It's not I who change the verses around and replace one verse with another—it is the Holy Spirit."

We know from the Bible that God doesn't change (Mal 3:6) or vacillate (Jas 1:17); therefore, Muhammad's revelation couldn't have been from God through the Holy Spirit (Mk 3:29) but came instead from the father of all lies. There is only one sin that cannot be forgiven: to blaspheme against the Holy Spirit (Mk 3:28-30). And though Muhammad is guilty of this sin, may God release and forgive Muhammad's followers as they put their trust in Jesus.

Since Muhammad was equivocating with his message, the inhabitants of Mecca became frustrated and angry with him and tried to kill him, surrounding him in one of Mecca's valleys. For three years, they laid siege to him and his followers, cutting off his food and supplies. Eventually, Muhammad and his followers escaped the siege of Mecca and fled toward the town of Yathrib (renamed "Medina"—literally, "the city").[26] This journey has become known as the Hijrah, and it initiated the beginning of the Islamic calendar.

During one very dark night, the opportunity for Muhammad's escape arose. He quietly crept between caves to avoid being tracked, and, like a criminal, he escaped the bounty his own tribe had put on his head before finally making it to Medina. Upon his arrival, he was grateful to find followers who had also successfully escaped the siege. Now refugees, they covenanted together to provide shelter and safety for one another and reminisced about the horrible stories of mistreatment by their own tribes back in Mecca. They longed to form a new community, claiming Allah was greater than all the tribes' pagan idols. But with such a small army and no money, they had no choice but to lay low and wait. However, with the charisma of Muhammad in their new city of Medina, they didn't have to wait long.

Day by day, Muhammad's numbers swelled with new followers and bands of mercenaries with whom he would raid caravans to finance his operations, taking plunder and captives to be used as slaves or ransom. However, the Jews in Medina refused to accept Muhammad as either a prophet or a messenger of God and would not follow him.

---

[26] Medina is located 270 miles due north of Mecca.

Stung by this rejection, Muhammad altered his message and changed his tactics. Instead of the peaceful means he'd learned from Waraka, he began to use force to accomplish his mission by subduing or slaughtering those who would oppose him. This included the merciless killing or eviction of all Jewish families and the enslaving of Jewish women as concubines for his troops, keeping only the most beautiful for himself. This response to his enemies marked a major shift in his theology, from one of peace to one of great and ruthless violence. Muslims today address this shift in their sacred writings called the "Doctrine of Abrogation."

JIHAD

The raids in Medina were the early beginnings of what is now known as *jihad* (dying for Allah while you kill an infidel, or unbeliever). Muhammad's love of jihad expanded once he gained control of Medina with his stronger forces; he used the spoils of war to fund his lavish lifestyle. Jihad is the most significant doctrine of Islam. It is the only guaranteed way into heaven—you *must* kill while you are being killed.

Muhammad now called for a reconquest of Mecca, the city that had cast him away. From that moment forward, he proclaimed Mecca as the religious center for his followers instead of Jerusalem; and for eight long years, he prepared to overthrow the city. This happened while his posture and doctrine underwent a radical change of focus from an attitude of peace to a disposition of war.

The Quranic verses speaking of jihad were added and greatly expanded once Muhammad returned and gained control of Mecca by means of a much larger and more powerful army. Now, Muslims were commanded to not just fight back when they were wronged or attacked, but to go on the offensive and kill all who were not subject to Allah. Specifically, they were to bring Christians and Jews into the submission of Islam or put them to death. This vital and fundamental concept of jihad gives the clearest understanding as to why terrorist attacks like 9/11 would be taught and encouraged directly from the Quran.

Consider the following passage, called "the verse of the sword," which most Muslim scholars, jihadists, and terrorists will use to justify their violent attacks:

> But when the sacred months are passed away, kill the idolaters (*non-Muslims*) wherever you may find them; and take them, and besiege them, and lie in wait for them in every place of observation (Quran 9:5).

This verse is said to annul the more than 114 other verses that prescribe less severe treatment for non-Muslims. The West knows this philosophy commanded by the Quran as Islamic terrorism, but Muslims know it simply as jihad, holy war. The idea of "terrorism" is also addressed in the Quran:

> Against them make ready your strength to the utmost of your power, including steeds of war, to strike **terror** into the hearts of the enemies, of Allah and your enemies, and others besides, whom you may not know, but whom Allah knows. Whatever you shall spend in the cause of Allah, shall be repaid unto you, and you shall not be treated unjustly (Quran 8:60).

Consider another disturbing admonition from the Quran:

> Indeed, the penalty for those who wage war against Allah and His Messenger and strive upon earth to cause corruption is none but that they be killed or crucified or that their hands and feet be cut off from opposite sides or that they be exiled from the land. That is for them a disgrace in this world; and for them in the Hereafter is a great punishment (Quran 5:33).

Does this sound like a religion of peace? Just by writing this book, I am considered an enemy of Allah and his messenger. According to this verse, Muslims must slaughter me in a most horrible manner, and many are more than willing to do so.

Another cruel response to those who don't believe is beheading. Quran 47:4 is the clear underpinning for the 21st century beheadings that have shocked the civilized world:

> And when you meet those who disbelieve, non-Muslims, while fighting in Jihad, cut off their heads until you have massacred them, and take them captive.

Quran 9:111 likewise states the same:

> Indeed, Allah has purchased from the believers their lives and their properties in exchange for that they will have Paradise. They fight in the cause of Allah, so they kill and are killed. It is a true promise binding upon Him in the Torah and the Gospel and the Quran. And who is truer to his covenant than Allah? So rejoice in your transaction which you have contracted. And it is that which is the great attainment.

How should we interpret this verse? One former Muslim, Nabeel Qureshi, who was the esteemed Christian author of *Answering Jihad: A Better Way Forward*, explains:

> Quran 9 is a command to disavow all treaties with polytheists and to subjugate Jews and Christians (9:29) so that Islam may "prevail over all religions" (9:33). It is fair to wonder whether any non-Muslims in the world are immune from being attacked, subdued or assimilated under this command. Muslims must fight, according to this final chapter of the Quran, and if they do not, then their faith is called into question, and they are counted among the hypocrites (9:44-45). If they do fight, they are promised one of two rewards, either spoils of war or heaven through martyrdom. Allah has made

a bargain with the mujahid who obeys: Kill or be killed in battle, and paradise awaits (9:111).[27]

This also clarifies why Osama bin Laden, a Saudi national, and his Islamic terrorists chose 9/11 for their attacks; it was to honor the Quran in Quran 9:111 which describes jihad as the only guaranteed way to heaven. Essentially, what Osama bin Laden accomplished on 9/11 was not only massacring nearly 3000 U.S. citizens, but also the creation of a perpetual reminder to Muslims that they must obey Quran 9:111 and give their lives as suicide bombers and terrorists. This is the highest calling for a Muslim. While Americans have memorials to commemorate 9/11, Muslims go to Quran 9:111 and teach their children that jihad is the reason for 9/11 and train them to do likewise.

Nowadays, jihad takes various shapes and forms. The most graphic form was evident on September 11, 2001: the widescale massacre of non-Muslims, exactly what ISIS[28] represents today. To see it more clearly, consider that the Saudi government has its own officially sanctioned army of mujahedeen (those engaged in jihad), commissioned to terrorize non-Muslims. This is an official department of the Saudi government, sanctioned under the Ministry of Interior.

Jihad may also take the less severe, more discrete form of online harassment, such as hacking websites of non-Muslims. This happened to our outreach organization website, meccatochrist.org. We posted a video of me sharing the Gospel in Mecca at the Kaaba while praying aloud in the name of Jesus. Within minutes, Muslim hackers attacked our website and

---

[27] Nabeel Qureshi. *Answering Jihad: A Better Way Forward* (Nashville: Zondervan, 2016), 42-54.
[28] ISIS is an acronym that means Islamic State in Iraq and Syria.

crashed our host server, taking down thousands of additional sites in the process.

In Islamic law, also known as Sharia, jihad is not a suggestion; it is a command for every follower of Allah. If a Muslim is not actively pursuing the death of infidels, he or she must at least continually pray for their deaths. This is in no way a religion of peace. It is illegal even to build a Christian church in the Kingdom of Saudi Arabia as reported recently in the Washington Times:

> On March 12, Sheik Abdul Aziz bin Abdullah, the grand mufti of Saudi Arabia, declared that it is "necessary to destroy all the churches of the region." The ruling came in response to a query from a Kuwaiti delegation over proposed legislation to prevent construction of churches in the emirate. The mufti based his decision on a story that on his deathbed, Muhammad declared, "There are not to be two religions in the [Arabian] Peninsula" [Al-Muwatta, Book 45, Hadith 18]. This passage has long been used to justify intolerance in the kingdom. Churches have always been banned in Saudi Arabia.[29]

PILLARS OF ISLAM

The pillars of Islam are held together by the belief in jihad. Apart from jihad, the only other pathway to heaven is by being a faithful Muslim, doing good deeds, etc. But heaven is not guaranteed. The good deeds of Sunni Islam are outlined by five pillars; without these pillars, one cannot be a Muslim at all.

The first pillar is to believe that there is only one God, Allah, and that Muhammad is his messenger. Known as Tawhid, this is the first pillar in almost all the sects of Islam. Muslims

---

[29] "Editorial: Destroy All Churches" (The Washington Times: Friday, March 16, 2012), accessed 28 February, 2018. https://www.washingtontimes.com/news/2012/mar/16/destroy-all-churches/

are proud of this declaration; but, unfortunately, they do not know its true meaning. When I was a Muslim, I thought I worshiped the one true God; but when Christ lifted the veil from my eyes, I realized that all Muslims are deceived. They bow down to the Kaaba, worshiping rocks in a black building. The Kaaba is built around a sacred black meteorite that Muslims believe was placed by Abraham and Ishmael in a corner of the Kaaba; they believe it's a symbol of God's covenant with Abraham and Ishmael, and, by extension, the Muslim community.

Muslim pilgrims worshiping at the Kaaba in Mecca

This practice of honoring the stones in the Kaaba is clearly borrowed from paganism but knit into the practice of Islam, contradicting exclusive monotheistic worship. What's more, the proclamation "Allahu Akbar" means "Allah is greater." This saying points to an earlier time when many gods were worshiped in the Gulf region; Allah was one of those gods, probably the moon god.[30] He is not proclaimed as simply great or the only god, but simply as the greater god. In contrast, when the Bible speaks of other gods, it declares them to be "no gods" (Deut 32:17), unmasking Islam's pagan roots.

The second pillar of Islam is to pray five times a day while facing Mecca. At the call to prayer, the whole city is overwhelmed with the ear-piercing command to pray booming over enormous loudspeakers. At the first call, which is before sunrise while everyone is asleep and at peace, the loud voices over the speakers disrupt the silent night in Mecca. It feels like the speaker is right next to your bed.

Throughout the day, everything shuts down at a call to prayer while the religious police patrol the city to make sure all businesses are closed, and every soul is present at the mosque. If you are not moving toward the mosque at the call to prayer, you will hear the religious police call to you through the speakers on their patrol cars, "Prayer! Prayer!" If you refuse to respond, they will stop you, shackle you, and drag you to the religious police station where you might be jailed or even whipped.

The third pillar is the poor tax (*zakat*: 2.5% of one's income). This donation is to be given directly to the local mosque after which the government of Saudi Arabia, via its official agency called the Ministry Office of Zakat, distributes the donations to various causes advancing Islam, including global Islamic terrorism as well as the ministry of *dawah*,[31] or Islamic evangelism. Additionally, zakat donations are used to

---

[30] Francis E. Peters, *Muhammad and the Origins of Islam*, (Albany, NY: SUNY Press, 1994), 109.
[31] Ministry of Islamic Evangelism, http://www.moia.gov.sa

bribe non-Muslims to convert to Islam as is instructed in the Quran (Quran 9:60).

The fourth pillar for every faithful Muslim is to celebrate the fast of Ramadan. During Ramadan, Muslims remember the initial giving of the Quran to Muhammad, and many Muslim families use this occasion to give gifts to one another, like a Muslim Christmas. The last day of Ramadan (when the fast is broken) was always my favorite day of the year because all my tribal relatives would shower me with financial gifts making me feel like the richest kid in the world.

The final pillar is to make a pilgrimage to the holy city of Mecca at least once in your lifetime. It's called *hajj*, and it has a specific day, time, and place. During the last month of the Islamic calendar, Muslims from all over the world—from every tribe, language, and race—would come to my city. The men would wear only white, unsewn and plain clothing—no undergarments or anything fitted. Perfumes are also prohibited. Once in Mecca, pilgrims would swarm the black Kaaba building, bow down to it, hang on its walls to receive blessings, and sacrifice livestock to receive the atonement that covers their sins. If the hajj is completed correctly, the pilgrims are forgiven and cleansed from sin, becoming as clean as the day they were born! During this time, my city would be overflowing with millions of people.

Throughout the rest of the Islamic year, Muslims would travel to Mecca to participate in something called *umrah*, a lesser pilgrimage to Mecca, to receive the blessing of Allah. When certain rituals are performed, such as circling the Kaaba and kissing the building that houses the black meteorite stone or drinking holy water called *Zam Zam*, the pilgrimage is believed to be effectual, readying the person for entrance into Paradise.

Sadly, even if one fulfills all his duties perfectly regarding the pillars, a faithful Muslim cannot be one hundred percent certain of Paradise. A Muslim must do as many good works as possible because he or she will be judged on whether or not their good works outweigh the bad on the Day of Judgment. No Muslim can be completely sure of entering Paradise on this path for human works are very uncertain and questionable. Since everyone falls short because of sin, no one is ever settled in their standing before Allah. This is one reason why many Muslims practice a rather obsessive-compulsive way of life, constantly repeating their good deeds because they are never sure if their works will prove good enough. It is an all-consuming way of life. For instance, many people pray more often than the required five times because if they do not fulfill the ceremonies of prayer precisely, a single misstep means their absolution is interrupted, their prayer is counted as sin, and they have to repeat the whole process again.

Most Muslims (75-85%) are Sunnis. The Shiite Muslims have the same pillars as Sunni Islam, but they add several more.[32] One additional pillar is the practice of Tabarra: expressing disassociation and hatred toward unbelievers.

In spite of all the good works a Muslim may do, the only sure way to heaven in Islam is through jihad: one's suicide while killing non-Muslims. At the end of the day, all the pillars

---

[32] For example, the official sixth pillar of the Shiite sect and the unofficial sixth pillar of Sunni Islam is Jihad. *Zakat* (annual required giving of 2.5%) is present in both, but in Shia there is an additional annual taxation, khoums (one-fifth of your unused income during the year). Khoums paid to the imams allow the religious leaders to acquire great wealth in a very short amount of time.

of Islam stand on the violent and ruthless foundation of jihad (Quran 9:111).

THE MUSLIM HOLY BOOKS

The Quran is compiled from the revelations given to Muhammad, and Muslims believe it is the word of God verbatim. The word "Quran" literally means "God said it." In Islam, the Quran is considered by Muslims to be the summary of the Old and New Testaments, and is superior to both according to Quran 5:48.

Early in its history, the Quran was passed on through oral recitation and committed to memory, not being formally written down until the rise of the third Caliph[33] of Islam, Uthman (d. 656 A.D.). During this time, the sacred text was at its greatest danger of being lost or changed as those who had memorized and recounted it had either died, misremembered, or been taught incorrectly. To ensure accuracy, Uthman gathered the existing manuscripts and wrote down his version of the Quran, the very one still read and taught today. So dedicated was Uthman to his version of the Quran that any manuscript differing from his was confiscated and burned.

Muslims have two lesser holy books collections called the Hadith and the Sunnah. The Hadiths are the compiled sayings of Muhammad which he would speak to the people in the mosque that they might memorize and, if possible, later write down. The Sunnah is a collection of teachings that refers to what Muhammad did. Both the Sunnah and the Hadith are subject to the authority of the Quran.

---

[33] The Caliph (literally "successor") is the chief Muslim civil and religious ruler, regarded as the successor of Muhammad.

SUNNIS & SHIITES & THEIR DIVERGENT TEACHINGS

Shortly after the death of Muhammad, two major sects of Islam arose: the Sunnis and the Shiites, opposing factions that arose from a family dispute for power. The Sunnis believe that Muhammad's successor should be someone who knew Muhammad intimately and would closely follow his teachings. On the other hand, Shiites contend that only someone who was in Muhammad's holy bloodline should lead the people of Islam. To this day, in Shiite circles, the descendants of Muhammad are honored and regarded as carriers of this holy bloodline.

Abubaker, the father-in-law of Muhammad through Muhammad's six-year-old bride, Aisha, was declared the first Caliph. However, Muhammad's cousin and son-in-law, Ali, desired to lead the Islamic faith in the Shiite tradition. This resulted in divergent teachings, disputed leaders, and constant wars between Muhammad's followers that continue even today.

Both Sunnis and Shiites follow the Quran of Uthman, but Sunnis follow one version of the Hadith while Shiites follow another.[34] Even the Syrian war that rages on as I write is a battle of control, a dispute over which writings are the most sacred.

The evil one wants to kill and destroy, and he has used the political aspirations and greed within Muhammad's family and companions to accomplish this at the cost of millions of

---

[34] Sunnis are more interested in following Abubaker (Muhammad's father-in-law) who did not recognize the descendants of Muhammad and focused on the teaching of Islam. The Shiites, on the other hand, are more interested in following Muhammad's cousin and son-in-law, Ali, who claimed to be part of the bloodline of Muhammad. The dispute between Shiite and Sunni Muslims has continued to be a struggle for power, money, and control over the spiritual and political center of Islam: Mecca.

souls over centuries. My family's tribe was not immune to this destruction. They are all Sunni Muslims, the same sect of Islam that has devoted themselves to radical terrorist groups such as the Taliban, ISIS, Hamas, and AQAP[35], among others.

FESTIVALS

Muslims celebrate two main festivals: Ramadan and the Festival of Sacrifice. Ramadan is the primary ritual of fasting in which all faithful Muslims forego food and drink throughout the daylight hours in the ninth month of the lunar calendar. At sunrise, the call to prayer goes out and the fast begins. For the houses that are too far away from the speakers of the mosques, there is a cannon that goes off before daylight, waking everyone for breakfast. By sunset, the fast has rendered everyone extremely hungry and thirsty, and the intense heat of Mecca serves only to compound the torment.

When at last the evening comes, families often gather together for a meal—typically dates and water, served on the ground—and wait eagerly to hear the roar of the cannon announcing the sunset and the breaking of the fast, releasing all to eat and drink. The last day of Ramadan is called *Eid al-Fitter* ("Festival of Fast Breaking"), on which the final breaking of the fast is celebrated and all rituals come to a close.

The second Muslim festival is *Eid al-Adha*, the Festival of Sacrifice. During the time of the hajj pilgrimage, Muslims all around sacrifice sheep and other livestock to cover their sins. Rivers of blood would flow through the streets and cover the city of Mecca on this day, spilling from altars upon which the sins of the people and their departed loved ones had by it been

---

[35] AQAP stands for "Al Qaeda in the Arabian Peninsula"

atoned. I can still hear my father saying, "This sacrifice is on behalf of our grandmothers and grandfathers." He would mention them by name as blood gushed forth from the sheep we'd offered.

I slaughtered my first sheep when I was just seven years old as part of my rite of passage into manhood. Doing so left me traumatized as the beloved sheep I had played with the day prior was the very sheep I was forced to kill! I watched it suffer, saw the tears coming from its eyes; my heart was shattered for I felt as though I had just betrayed a dear friend. But I couldn't show that. I wanted to cry, but I had to hold it in so that I would be considered a man among my brothers and preserve my place of honor.

Vividly, I recall stepping upon the sheep while my brother placed the cold steel of the knife into my hand. I was shaking. And then, having spotted me from far away trembling before my brothers, my mother screamed, "Be a man like your brothers!"

I forced myself to kill the sheep. I tried to look strong on the outside, but inside I was crushed.

The practice of animal sacrifice for atonement is quite familiar to Christians and Jews. Islam has copied so many of the Old Testament traditions and rituals as well, including animal sacrifice. How empty is this sacrifice, however, if atonement is expected from a mere animal! "Under the old system, the blood of goats and bulls and the ashes of a heifer could cleanse people's bodies from ceremonial impurity. Just think how much more the blood of Christ will purify our consciences from sinful deeds so that we can worship the living God. For by the power of the eternal Spirit, Christ offered himself to God as a perfect sacrifice for our sins" (Heb 9:13-14).

Islam has not changed significantly since its beginnings. So, let us now consider how Muhammad's teachings still influence people today in Mecca and around the world.

Appendix 2 | ISLAM TODAY

Satan, who is the god of this world, has blinded the minds of those who don't believe. They are unable to see the glorious light of the Good News. They don't understand this message about the glory of Christ, who is the exact likeness of God."
2 CORINTHIANS 4:4

Saudi Arabia represents the heart of the Muslim world. It is the only country on earth that has their religious declaration of faith written on their national flag.

The flag reads: "There is no God but Allah and Muhammad is his messenger." Beneath this statement of faith is the sword representing the punishment for anyone found defying this statement: death by decapitation. Indeed, the national anthem of Saudi Arabia supports the message of the flag:

To glory and supremacy,
Glorify the Creator of the heavens!
And raise the green flag
Carrying the written light reflecting guidance,
Repeat: Allahu Akbar! (Allah is greater!)
O my country!
My country,
Live as the pride of Muslims!
Long live the King
For the flag
And the homeland!

Of all the Arabian countries, Saudi Arabia adheres most closely to the literal intent of the Quran which is lived out through the Sharia law. My culture and my father's daily teaching in the mosque have given me many insights into the belief system and structure of the Islam that I grew up with. What I am about to describe is not the experience of all Muslims. Islam is not monolithic. Much of Islam around the world is quite moderate and mild. But the version of Islam I grew up with in Saudi Arabia is the most strict and extreme, called Wahhabism.

NO RELIGIOUS FREEDOM

In Saudi Arabia, there is no freedom of religion at all. The Grand Mufti of Saudi Arabia (like a Muslim pope) has publicly stated his intention to destroy all churches. As of this moment, there are no official Christian meeting places anywhere in Saudi. From the Huffington Post, April 12, 2012:

> Saudi Arabia's highest Islamic authority, Sheikh Abdul Aziz bin Abdullah, made the inflammatory comments in response to a question from a Kuwaiti delegation which asked about a Kuwaiti parliamentarian's call to get rid of all churches there.
>
> Abdullah said it is "necessary to destroy all the churches in the region. There are not to be two religions in the Arabian Peninsula."[36]

No church meeting places may exist in Saudi Arabia, and it is illegal for citizens of Saudi Arabia or any Gulf State (Bahrain, Iraq, Kuwait, Oman, Qatar, Saudi Arabia, and the United Arab Emirates, or UAE) to be a Christian. According to the U.S. Department of State's *International Religious Freedom Report for 2016 for Saudi Arabia*, Section II, "Conversion from Islam to another religion is grounds for the charge of apostasy, a crime which is legally punishable by death."[37] The U.S. Commission on International Religious Freedom reported in 2017: "The Saudi government continues to use criminal charges of apostasy and blasphemy to suppress debate and silence dissidents."[38] Even atheism is considered terrorism in Saudi Arabia.[39]

Saudi law also forbids all non-Muslims from entering

---

[36] Simon McCormack. "Sheikh Abdul Aziz Bin Abdullah, Saudi Islamic Leader, Says Churches Should Be Destroyed" (Washington DC: Huffington Post, 4/02/2012), https://www.huffingtonpost.com/2012/04/02/sheikh-abdul-aziz-bin-abdullah-says-churches-should-be-destroyed_n_1398157.html. Accessed 3/9/2018.

[37] Bureau of Democracy, Human Rights and Labor. "International Religious Freedom Report for 2016, Saudi Arabia, Section II" (Washington DC: U.S. Department of State, 2016). Accessed 3/8/2018. https://www.state.gov/j/drl/rls/irf/religiousfreedom/index.htm?year=2016&dlid=268912#wrapper.

[38] Erin D. Singshinsuk. "Annual Report on the U.S. Commission on International Religious Freedom" (Washington DC: USCIRF, April 2017), http://www.uscirf.gov/sites/default/files/2017.USCIRFAnnualReport.pdf. Accessed 3/9/2018.

[39] Ibid.

Mecca. As you approach the "holy city," giant signs and checkpoints warn that only Muslims may enter Mecca.

WOMEN

In Islam, women have almost no rights whatsoever. Until recently, they could not even drive or travel without a husband's or male guardian's permission. For example, if a woman has no husband or father, she may have to ask her ten-year-old son or relative for permission to leave the house, go shopping, or even get married! Muslim women are viewed as mere shadows and as property. Historically, they have been treated like any other spoil of battle and used in many ways: sexual pleasure, reproduction, or even bought and sold as slaves and concubines. This has, in part, aided the expansion of Islam through the centuries at the grave cost of degrading women.

Islam also teaches that women are deficient in their intellect. The most trusted Hadith, documented by Sahih al-Bukhari, tells this story:

> The women asked, 'O Allah's Messenger! What is deficient in our intelligence and religion?' He said, 'Is not the evidence of two women equal to the witness of one man?' They replied in the affirmative. He said, 'This is the deficiency in her intelligence. Isn't it true that a woman can neither pray nor fast during her menstrual cycle?' The women replied in the affirmative. He said, 'This is the deficiency in her religion.'
> *Sahih al-Bukhari, Book 6, Hadith 301*

Al-Bukhari has also recorded a story in which Muhammad compares women to dogs and donkeys: "The prayer is severed by a woman, a dog and a donkey" (Sahih al-Bukhari, Book 22, Hadith 492).

To add further insult, it is said that women are the predominant people in hell because of their inherent ungratefulness.

> The Messenger of Allah said: 'I was shown Hell and I have never seen anything more terrifying than it. And I saw that the majority of its people are women.' They said, 'Why, O Messenger of Allah?' He said, 'Because of their ingratitude [*kufr*].' It was said, 'Are they ungrateful to Allah?' He said, 'They are ungrateful to their companions [husbands] and ungrateful for good treatment. If you are kind to one of them for a lifetime then she sees one [undesirable] thing in you, she will say, 'I have never had anything good from you.'
> *Sahih al-Bukhari, Book 16, Hadith 12*

Even in Islam's version of heaven, women do not have as much pleasure as men. A woman's reward in heaven is merely joining the husband she had on earth while men are given numerous beautiful, heavenly virgins. The *houris* (heavenly virgins) are beings in Islam described in English translations as "full-breasted companions of equal age," "lovely eyed," and of "modest gaze." Such heavenly virgins are creatures found only in the Islamic heaven (Quran 44:54; 52:20; 55:72; 56:22; 78:33).

How does this compare to the way we see Christ treat women in the New Testament? In Scripture, Christ dignifies women. He speaks to the Samaritan woman at the well and reveals to her, an adulteress, that he is the Messiah. She, in turn, becomes the first missionary of the Gospel (Jn 4). Instead of stoning a woman caught in adultery, he offered her mercy and compassion, telling her, "Go, and sin no more" (Jn 8:11). When Jesus rose from the dead, he didn't reveal himself to his male disciples; he thought that the testimony of a woman was valid enough to prove his resurrection (Mt 28:1-10). And God sent Christ into this world via the womb of a woman: Mary the mother of Jesus (Lk 1:42-43). In the book of Galatians, it clearly states that there is no male or female; we are all one in Christ (Gal 3:28). This attitude of equality and compassion toward women is consistently found in the actions of Christ.

WIFE BEATING

Marriage in Islam is not about having a relationship and sharing love. Rather, it is about a marital contract that includes sex, reproduction, keeping house, and raising children. A Muslim husband can divorce his wife for any reason, such as barrenness, failure to maintain a clean household, any slight disobedience, inability to provide sexual pleasure, or whatever else the husband desires.

An obvious lack of love is present in Muslim marriages as Muhammad permits husbands to beat their wives. In fact, instructions to do so are found in the Quran (4:34; 38:34) and the Hadith:

> The Prophet said: A man will not be asked as to why he beat his wife.
> *Sunan Abi Dawud, Book 9, Hadith 1986*

Many times, while working in the medical field in Saudi Arabia, I would be presented with cases of women who had been repeatedly beaten. Once, as a member of an emergency response team, I entered a home immediately after the police had broken down the door. There I was confronted with the body of a woman lying on the ground. Unresponsive, covered in bruises, and bleeding profusely, she had been severely and savagely beaten by her husband; but the police did not ask the man a single question as per the Hadith. I cried out to the Lord on her behalf, but there was no means of justice for her within the teaching of Islam. All I could do was bandage her wounds and pray; but, even as I did so, I knew that once she recovered, she would be forced to return to the same man who had beaten her almost to the point of death.

And again, women must have permission from a male guardian to do anything, even if it is her ten-year-old relative. The Human Rights Watch reports:

> Saudi Arabia's male guardianship system remains the most significant impediment to women's rights in the country despite limited reforms over the last decade. Adult women must obtain permission from a male guardian to travel abroad, marry, or be released from prison, and may be required to provide guardian consent to work or get health care. These restrictions last from birth until death, as women are, in the view of the Saudi state, permanent legal minors. Women in Saudi Arabia face formal and informal barriers when attempting to make decisions or take action without the presence or consent of a male relative. As one 25-year-old Saudi woman told Human Rights Watch, "We all have to live in the borders of the boxes our dads or husbands draw for us." In some cases, men use the permission requirements to extort large sums of money from female dependents.[40]

The story goes on to say that husbands are free to beat their wives. In the Kingdom of Saudi Arabia, the Quran allows wife beating; and, therefore, there is no accountability for men.

Women may be sent to prison if they do not obey their husbands. This too isolates and humiliates women, especially those who would try to insist on their human rights.

> Women who have escaped abuse in shelters may, and in prisons do, require a male relative to agree to their release. "The

---

[40] "Saudi Arabia: Male Guardianship Boxes Women In Restricts Movement, Work, Health, Safety" (Beirut, Lebanon: Human Rights Watch, July 16, 2016) Accessed 3/16/2018. Web: www.hrw.org/news/2016/07/16/saudi-arabia-male-guardianship-boxes-women

[authorities] keep a woman in jail… until her legal guardian comes and gets her, even if he is the one who put her in jail," said a women's rights activist. If a guardian refuses to release a woman from prison, authorities may transfer her to a state shelter or arrange a marriage for her. Her new husband becomes her new guardian.[41]

The love of Christ is the only hope for women in Islam, who, like all Muslims, have never experienced true biblical love. In Islam, there are ninety-nine known names of God, and not one of them is Love (1 Jn 4:8). Nor can any description of self-sacrificial love, as in 1 Corinthians 13, be found in its teachings. Christ gave himself up as a loving sacrifice for his bride (Eph 5:25). When the Jewish police came to get Jesus, he chose not to put his disciples in danger; rather, he put himself in danger for their sake. Jesus is the good shepherd, and he gave his life for his flock. There is no greater love than this (Jn 15:13).

The actions of Christ are the exact opposite of Muhammad's who would make his students/disciples defend him and fight to the death that he might be spared in the midst of war (Quran 9:29). Perhaps this is the greatest difference between Islam and Christianity: a disciple in Islam has a relationship comparable to that of a slave serving a loveless master. But a disciple in Christianity has a relationship comparable to that of a son or daughter to a devoted father, grounded in love and friendship.

POLYGAMY

According to some Islamic reports, Muhammad married more than twelve women, but a Muslim may not have more

---

[41] Ibid.

than four wives. However, Muslim men are allowed an unlimited number of concubines. Think of it! A man's concubine is just a girlfriend on the side with whom he has no children and fulfills only his sexual desires. Polygamy is not much better. When my father preaches in the mosque about polygamy, he might address it from the Quran using Quran 4:3 which says,

> And if you fear that you cannot act equitably toward orphans, then marry such women as seem good to you, two and three and four; but if you fear that you will not do justice between them, then marry only one or what your right hands possess [your right hand possesses slaves]; this is more proper, that you may not deviate from the right course.

Perhaps a simpler way to rephrase this Quranic verse can be found in the words my father taught me. He would often preach in the mosque saying, "You can marry up to four women, but why not get yourself a sex slave so you can have unlimited sex?"

This brings up the obvious question: Why would Muhammad not follow what his god had said regarding marriage? As has already been mentioned, Muhammad had up to ten wives at a time. The answer is that Muhammad did not follow his own Quran.

SLAVERY

Slavery is widely practiced in Islam throughout many Arabian countries, including Saudi Arabia. Technically, slavery in Saudi Arabia has been illegal since its abolition in 1962 following massive international pressure. The Saudi royals publicly declare that slavery is illegal, but Saudis privately continue to own slaves. Most of the slaves come from Africa, have no freedoms, are castrated to ensure they remain obedient, and are never allowed to be near their master's wives.

With respect to slavery and human trafficking, Saudi Arabia was put on the Tier 2 watchlist by the U.S. State Department in its *2017 Trafficking in Persons Report*. The Tier 2 watchlist includes "countries whose governments do not fully meet the TVPA's minimum standards and...the trafficking number victims are very significant or significantly increasing."[42]

In Saudi Arabia and other Gulf States, there are millions of foreigners who come to these Muslim countries to find work as house servants, construction workers, and other service-related jobs, only to end up in modern-day slavery. The master of the house is obligated by law to hold the foreign worker's passport, essentially turning that foreigner into the master's property. They often work with no income or return for their service, apart from receiving food and a place to sleep, and they may never be able to return to their homeland. Yet, the worst kind of slavery goes beyond mere household servitude and into the realm of sex slavery, encouraged in the Quran as previously described.

Muhammad's thirst for unlimited sex and sexual slaves is shockingly justified by the Quran's "revelation from Allah" found in Quran 33:50, 4:3 and other passages which allow for sex slaves. These passages refer to having sex with "what your right hand possesses," a metaphor for a household slave. In other words, the teaching of the Quran is that a man may turn any household slave into his personal sex slave.

---

[42] U.S. State Department. *Office to Monitor and Combat Trafficking in Persons.* (Washington DC: Tier Placements, 2017), http://state.gov/j/tip/rls/tiprpt/2017/271117.htm. Accessed 1 Jan 2018.

MUSIC FORBIDDEN

The Quran forbids music. Quran 31:5 says,

> And of mankind is he who purchases idle talks (i.e. music, singing, etc.) to mislead people from the path of Allah without knowledge, and takes the path of Allah by way of mockery. For such there will be a humiliating torment in the hellfire.

I remember one time when I was a child, I saw a "Made in China" instrument on my way to the mosque. It was like a flute, but it had a square structure, and I had no idea how it functioned. Unwittingly, I picked it up from the dirty ground just as a strong wind rushed past me, blowing into the instrument and producing a beautiful sound. Those who heard it dragged me away to the mosque where my feet were beaten (i.e. *falaka*) in front of everyone. Even as an adult, to avoid the sound of music, I programmed my phone to chant an Islamic poem instead of a ring.

There are musicians in Saudi Arabia, but they are considered secular and nonreligious, and they have been oppressed for a long time. Forty years ago, there was an "awakening" in which the people embraced a more extreme version of Islam. Before this, people were very interested in the arts. There was music, movie theatres, etc. Saudi women were permitted to drive cars and didn't have to cover their heads or bodies! After this so-called awakening, however, most of the Saudi musicians fled to nearby countries, and the restrictions against women increased. Today, if anyone is found playing a musical instrument in public, the religious police will come, confiscate it, and perform an "execution" on the musical instrument by thoroughly destroying it. Additionally, anyone raised under

Sharia law is forbidden to have a television in the house as it is looked upon as the mediator of Satan.

As Christians, we believe that music is a sacred and powerful tool for worshiping God. But Satan cunningly twists these beautiful creations to influence people, either to reject them or use them for evil purposes. Christians, on the other hand, use God's gift of music to express a form of worship mere words cannot convey. God has given man an entire book of 150 Psalms that can be sung in congregational worship. Jesus himself sang a hymn at the conclusion of the Last Supper. "Then they sang a hymn and went out to the Mount of Olives" (Mt 26:30).

THE DEATH PENALTY: BEHEADING, CRUCIFIXION, ETC.

Capital crimes in Saudi Arabia include apostasy (leaving Islam), atheism, treason against the king, murder, rape, drug smuggling, blasphemy, burglary, adultery (unmarried adulterers can be sentenced to 100 lashes; married ones can be sentenced to stoning), sodomy, homosexuality, lesbianism, etc.

Usually, the death penalty is issued by the courts which are led by imams or muftis, and the official sentence is typically decapitation by sword in the town square in accordance with Muhammad's commands. Every Friday, these sentences and others, such as cutting off a hand or a foot, are carried out. Doctors are stationed nearby, waiting to sew up the appendages of traumatized lawbreakers. Sometimes the sentence of crucifixion is given, either to torture a condemned individual before death or to display a body postmortem. Once all those sentenced to death have died, their corpses are hung from a high crane, visible for miles around, so that the entire community can see what befalls those who defy the rules.

There is also an unofficial death penalty, carried out by radical Muslims or the family of a disobedient member. It is a great shame to the community if a person abandons Islam for other teachings, and it is considered a restoration of the community's honor if the father kills his apostate son or daughter. Although this is murder, the father faces no penalty. Even if police come to investigate, such cases are dismissed at the scene without further questioning because what has occurred is considered an honor killing in Islam, also known as "washing of the shame." When family members, or their communities, take such actions, they believe they are doing a holy service to God and to Islam.

In a country like the United States where Sharia law does not exist, a fatwa (a ruling by a Muslim judge regarding a region outside Islam) may be enforced. Fatwas may be issued by Muslim states, individual Islamic judges, or leaders "demanding the death of the apostate, using the statement, 'his blood is permissible.' Individual fatwas...can be acted upon by any Muslim, and many would argue that an assassin is obeying Sharia law and must not be prosecuted."[43]

Finally, murder for apostasy may be done in an even more underhanded fashion. If a person has violated Islam, the religious police or radical Muslims sometimes plot to stealthily kill that person as in the case of Jamal Ahmad Khashoggi, a Saudi Arabian dissident, author, and columnist for *The Washington Post*. These deaths take place without a court sentence and are used to make the victim an example, striking terror

---

[43] Patrick Sookhdeo. *Freedom to Believe: Challenging Islam's Apostasy Law* (McLean, VA: Isaac Publishing, 2009).

into the hearts of the community. "The perpetrators are rarely prosecuted by the authorities and frequently go unpunished. Some Muslim states worry about the unwelcome attention given by the Western media to cases of apostasy, so they prefer to let such cases be handled unofficially by the family or community."[44]

MY DEVOTION TO ISLAM

Until I was 19 years old, I was sincerely devoted to Islam. I faithfully followed, studied, and supported the teachings of Islam as related above. Islam means to surrender or to submit. Instead of being surrendered to a loving, compassionate God, I was surrendered to the view of a god who urged me to hate unbelievers and sinners, and that fruit was evident in my life. I hated Christians and Jews as I had been taught by the Quran to do. I trusted in Islam's god and prophet without a doubt and with full devotion. It never came to my mind that one day I would follow Jesus Christ and become the so-called "infidel" I had always hated. I testify with Paul:

> Whatever gain I had, I counted as loss for the sake of Christ. Indeed, I count everything as loss because of the surpassing worth of knowing Christ Jesus my Lord. For his sake I have suffered the loss of all things and count them as rubbish, in order that I may gain Christ and be found in him, not having a righteousness of my own that comes from the law, but that which comes through faith in Christ, the righteousness from God that depends on faith—that I may know him and the power of his resurrection, and may share his sufferings, becoming like him in his death... (Phil 3:7-10, ESV).

---

[44] Ibid.

ACKNOWLEDGEMENTS

This book would not have been possible without an army of people who helped in the process of writing this book. None wanted to be named, but I am so grateful to the brother who transcribed the first rough draft of this book as I dictated it to him. He urged me to begin writing while I was still living in Saudi Arabia, and we spent days and nights over the phone birthing a written record of timelines, stories, histories, and events of how God has moved in my life. Later, when I arrived in the U.S., we spent many nights in his office having "red eye" sessions through the night as we discussed how to express certain ideas in English. I am also indebted to my editor who carefully reworked the entire transcript so that it would flow more smoothly. There were several people who carefully looked over the transcript and helped revise it. To all those who spent countless days and hours working tirelessly on the production of this book, I say, "Thank you!"

In his kindness God called you to share in his eternal glory by means of Christ Jesus. So, after you have suffered a little while, he will restore, support, and strengthen you, and he will place you on a firm foundation. All power to him forever! Amen.
1 Peter 5:10-11

SOLI DEO GLORIA

www.ingramcontent.com/pod-product-compliance
Lightning Source LLC
Chambersburg PA
CBHW071231080526
44587CB00013BA/1566